Therapiece Workbook
Mar-2023

Therapiece Workbook

In January 2019 the Therapiece pilot group met for the first time.

Therapiece pilot 11-Jul-19 : The Therapiece Logo was adopted.

In January 2020 the pilot group turn in to a formal group and expanded due to demand.
In April 2020 the first general meeting took place. A formal small society with not for profit "social enterprise" aspirations was formed in November 2020.

Therapiece Annual General Meetings were held in November 2021 and December 2022.

To find out more about Therapiece then take a look at
https://therapiece.org

Acknowledgements
The cover of this book and the Therapiece logo is based on a painting by George Tooker
MASKED BALL - Un Ballo in Maschera

The cover is blurred to retain the colours. This painting is in the public domain and the acknowledgement is given here.

First published as
ISBN: 9798385845378

Copyright statement.

Authors & Contributors: Therapiece is a peer-to-peer network of people, a small society or group. This workbook is based on work between 2019 and 2022. Please find a list of people who have contributed to this Workbook here:-

https://therapiece.org/workbook-2022-contributors/

Others joined Therapiece also contributed but do not appear in this workbook or in the list. Some of the list do not appear as authors but contributed in other ways

Workbook Content

_

Introduction to the Therapiece Workbook

The Therapiece Workbook has two main aims:-

- To act as a reference for anyone who has been or wants to take part in therapeutic writing based on the Therapiece model

- To celebrate the achievement of setting up Therapiece and also enable others to follow the same path.

There is quite a lot of evidenced based work which supports what is behind Therapiece – this Workbook looks at a practical way to turn that theory into a regular activity for a group of people. There are a number of key aspects to this including how to engender and preserve trust.

This is the first edition and may well be the only version; but if the Therapiece organisation continues to be sustainable and successful then this could be followed up with subsequent editions.

The Workbook is laid out as a series of sheets which can also be used as quick reference – blank pages are included to preserve this and for your own notes.

Therapiece Aims & Ethos

Here, we explore what it means to be a Therapiece member.

How is the Therapiece approach different from other writing groups you might have been in before?

What practices will we use to share and communicate with during Therapiece sessions?

How will we keep ourselves and our fellow members safe?

What Is Therapiece?

Therapiece is a project aimed at encouraging creativity within a therapeutic framework. Based on peer-to-peer principles, "equal time" and "author in charge," the group will be geared towards helping people meet their emotional needs and strengthen their human resources, while using their creative processes like writing and art.

Think of Therapiece as a network of people with the aim of linking creativity with emotions that will help exercise and relax their mind muscle.

Aims

What could the aims be of a creative group within a therapeutic framework? The simple art of expressing oneself. Making marks on paper to share with others. To be truly seen and heard, without judgement. To explore or discover aspects of ourselves that we may have either hidden or defended against or which are unfamiliar to us. To integrate and accept these aspects. To experiment with storytelling, imagination, metaphor, and stream of consciousness as a way of exploring both our creativity and our thoughts and feelings. To be informed/inspired/opened up by others – through their stories, methods, beliefs, ways of being. A present moment process, with immediacy; raw and real, where the end result is of lesser significance than the experiencing, where it feels as if something has changed or released, where whatever is current has been expressed. To be part of a group – learning to experience sharing, participating, supporting, leading, following, trusting, being open, being ourselves. To spawn new ideas and increase creativity. To enjoy ourselves.

Golden Rules

- **Equal time.** Every participant will get the same amount of time with which to share their piece.

- **Author in charge.** Authors will outline their "contract" at the start of the session, guiding readers in what kind of questions and feedback they welcome.

- **Reflective listening.** During each member's feedback session, a culture of respect is vital. Ask questions based on what you've heard rather than commenting. Avoid comforting.

- **Non-judgmental contributions.** Feedback and questions should avoid judgement and assumption, also avoid life advice, but can include positive reader reactions.

- **Self-responsibility.** To support others, ensure you are well enough to attend the session and able to give your full attention.

- **Rotating who provides the prompt.** Meeting prompts and themes will be selected by group members on a rotating basis and should not contain writing by anyone in the group. Anyone who is not confident to present a prompt can still put one forward for someone in the group to present.

- **No intoxication.** There will be a zero-tolerance policy for intoxication (alcohol or recreational drugs) at meetings.

- **Confidentiality.** Anything discussed in the group stays in the group.

- **Speaking up.** If you feel the Golden Rules are being broken, please raise this at the time or in the group feedback.

- **Safeguarding.** If you feel unsafe or need assistance, you can find the Therapiece Safeguarding Process here https://therapiece.org/members-safeguarding/

More details looking at the intention of these rules are given in the "Extra pages" section.

Membership and Joining

- Therapiece will be open to all who write in English.

- Members are expected to uphold the Golden Rules (and to remind each other if necessary).

- Members are expected to engender "the safe feeling" of the group, including practicing confidentiality and non-judgemental contributions.

- New members may attend two meetings before they formally join the group by affirming that they will stick to the group rules and ethos.

Issue 2.2 Nov-2022

Therapiece Writing in the Moment

Therapiece Ethos - Golden Rules

**Writing in the Moment has the same
structure as art in the Moment**

- **Equal time.** Every participant will get the same amount of time with which to share their piece.

- **Author in charge.** Authors will outline their "contract" at the start of the session, guiding readers in what kind of questions and feedback they welcome.

- **Reflective listening.** During each member's feedback session, a culture of respect is vital. Ask questions based on what you've heard rather than commenting. Avoid comforting.

- **Non-judgmental contributions.** Feedback and questions should avoid judgement and assumption, also avoid life advice, but can include positive reader reactions.

- **Self-responsibility.** To support others, ensure you are well enough to attend the session and able to give your full attention.

- **A rotating prompt.** Meeting prompts and themes will be selected by group members on a rotating basis and should not contain writing by anyone in the group.

- **No intoxication.** There will be a zero-tolerance policy for intoxication (alcohol or recreational drugs) at meetings.

- **Confidentiality.** Anything discussed in the group stays in the group.

- **Speaking up.** If you feel the Golden Rules are being broken, please raise this at the time or in the group feedback.

- **Safeguarding.** If you feel unsafe or need assistance, you can find the Therapiece Safeguarding Process here https://therapiece.org/members-safeguarding/

More details looking at the intention of these rules are given in the "Extra pages" section.

Meeting Structure

1. **Opening "circle"** (equal time - discussion of expectations, contract/interventions) 1:30mins
2. **Prompt.** Description of the writing prompt for writing in the moment - 5mins
3. **Writing in the Moment** – 20 mins shared time
4. **Author time** the writing or experience (need not share what you have written) - 12 mins each
5 **Attention switch** if requested
6 After everyone has completed 4 & 5 :- **Feedback & Closing circle.**

If there are five participants in the group, we will break at an agreed time for 5-10 minutes each hour.

If there are six or more in the group, author time will be done in two or more sub-groups – all coming together afterwards for Feedback / Closing Circle.

Free attention and Listening

What does it mean to *listen* using free attention in a WiM session?

- Listen to the author's contract – if they do not state one, assume a "normal contract"
- Be interested in what you're hearing, but not necessarily responsive to it
- Maintain a friendly expression without smiling, nodding or saying anything, just a willingness to listen
- It is ok not to ask questions and not to have time to ask your question
- There doesn't (always) have to be a solution
- Sometimes things just change, i.e. you do not have to be goal oriented
- All of this can be beneficial to the listener as well as the author

Contracts and Contributions

A contract, often established during the Opening Circle or at the start of the Authors time, is made by the author and presented to the group. It provides guidance on what kind of contributions and interventions the writer wants that day.

Providing a contract allows the writer to create their own boundaries, protecting themselves from unwanted kinds of feedback and maintaining autonomy. A contribution (usually called intervention in co-counselling) is an offering from another group member or reader.

An example of a contract could be: "Today I would like contributions/feedback on the emotional impact of my writing, but first I would like to explore my own feelings about the issue I present in the piece. I would like listeners to wait until I say that I'm ready for that feedback."

Or: "Today I would like to experiment with not being asked questions. Instead I would like to simply experience free attention after I read my piece."

A "normal contract" would be a mix of free attention and one or two contributions, including statements of positive enjoyment.

One perceived benefit of these kinds of contracts is a focus on process over product/performance. They allow the reader to share and receive external input, see what emerges, be surprised, but also to be present in the moment and let go of tight control over the results of their creativity.

Here are some examples of contributions that might work:
> General
>> Has anything changed since you wrote this?
>> What will you take forward into your writing from today?
>> Is there a piece of 'treasure' in your writing? Something you would like to follow up?
> Feelings
>> What does X (some element or object of the writing) mean to you?
>> How did the process (of writing / reviewing) make you feel?
>> How are you feeling now?
>> What is conspicuous by its absence in your writing?
>> Which part of the story do you like the most? And why?
> Follow-up
>> As a result of your writing do you want to make an action plan or make a new goal?
>> Is there anything else you want to say or explore? Tell me more!

Group Feedback

Each member has equal time (usually 1:30 min) to give their feedback about any aspect of how the meeting has gone for them.

- Would I do it differently next time - e.g. choose a different contract?
- Did it help? Did I enjoy it? What have I learnt?
- Did the meeting follow the Therapiece ethos and encourage creativity?
- What could my Listeners have done differently?
- Is there anything I can celebrate or appreciate about my session?

At the end of the feedback the meeting usually ends – if there have been some issues about Safeguarding or the Ethos then sometimes it can be useful to have a short discussion of the rules or their interpretation.

Issue 2.2 Jun-2022

Therapiece Art in the Moment

Therapiece Ethos - Golden Rules

Art in the Moment   structure follows
the writing in the moment

- **Equal time.** Every participant will get the same amount of time with which to share their piece.

- **Creator in charge.** Artists will outline their "contract" at the start of the session, guiding readers in what kind of questions and feedback they welcome.

- **Reflective listening.** During each member's feedback session, a culture of respect is vital. Ask questions based on what you've heard rather than commenting. Avoid comforting.

- **Non-judgmental contributions.** Feedback and questions should avoid judgement and assumption, also avoid life advice, but can include positive reader reactions.

- **Self-responsibility.** To support others, ensure you are well enough to attend the session and able to give your full attention.

- **A rotating prompt.** Meeting prompts and themes will be selected by group members on a rotating basis and should not contain material by anyone in the group.

- **No intoxication.** There will be a zero-tolerance policy for intoxication (alcohol or recreational drugs) at meetings.

- **Confidentiality.** Anything discussed in the group stays in the group.

- **Speaking up.** If you feel the Golden Rules are being broken, please raise this at the time or in the group feedback.

- **Safeguarding.** If you feel unsafe or need assistance, you can find the Therapiece Safeguarding Process here https://therapiece.org/members-safeguarding/

More details looking at the intention of these rules are given in the "Extra pages" section.

Meeting Structure

1. **Opening "circle"** (equal time - discussion of expectations, contract/interventions) 1:30mins
2. **Prompt.** Description of the writing prompt for writing in the moment - 5mins
3. **Art in the Moment** – 20 mins shared time
4. **Artist time** the art or experience (no not share what you have created) - 12 mins each
5 **Attention switch** if requested
6 After everyone has completed 4 & 5 :- **Feedback & Closing circle.**

If there are five participants in the group, we will break at an agreed time for 5-10 minutes each hour.

If there are six or more in the group, author time will be done in two or more sub-groups – all coming together afterwards for Feedback / Closing Circle.

Free attention and Listening

What does it mean to *listen* using free attention in a AiM session?

- Listen to the author's contract – if they do not state one, assume a "normal contract"

- Be interested in what you're hearing, but not necessarily responsive to it

- Maintain a friendly expression without smiling, nodding or saying anything, just a willingness to listen

- It is ok not to ask questions and not to have time to ask your question

- There doesn't (always) have to be a solution

- Sometimes things just change, i.e. you do not have to be goal oriented

- All of this can be beneficial to the listener as well as the author

Contracts and Contributions

A contract, often established during the Opening Circle or at the start of the Authors time, is made by the author and presented to the group. It provides guidance on what kind of contributions and interventions the writer wants that day.

Providing a contract allows the writer to create their own boundaries, protecting themselves from unwanted kinds of feedback and maintaining autonomy. A contribution (usually called intervention in co-counselling) is an offering from another group member or reader.

An example of a contract could be: "Today I would like contributions/feedback on the emotional impact of my writing, but first I would like to explore my own feelings about the issue I present in the piece. I would like listeners to wait until I say that I'm ready for that feedback."

Or: "Today I would like to experiment with not being asked questions. Instead I would like to simply experience free attention after I read my piece."

A "normal contract" would be a mix of free attention and one or two contributions, including statements of positive enjoyment.

One perceived benefit of these kinds of contracts is a focus on process over product/performance. They allow the reader to share and receive external input, see what emerges, be surprised, but also to be present in the moment and let go of tight control over the results of their creativity.

Here are some examples of contributions that might work:
> General
>> Has anything changed since you created this?
>> What will you take forward into your work from today?
>> Is there a piece of 'treasure' in your work? Something you would like to follow up?
> Feelings
>> What does X (some element or object of the art) mean to you?
>> How did the process (of creating / reviewing) make you feel?
>> How are you feeling now?
>> What is conspicuous by its absence in your piece?
>> Which part of your work do you like the most? And why?
> Follow-up
>> As a result of your work do you want to make an action plan or make a new goal?
>> Is there anything else you want to say or explore? Tell us more!

Group Feedback

Each member has equal time (usually 1:30 min) to give their feedback about any aspect of how the meeting has gone for them.

- Would I do it differently next time - e.g. choose a different contract?
- Did it help? Did I enjoy it? What have I learnt?
- Did the meeting follow the Therapiece ethos and encourage creativity?
- What could my Listeners have done differently?
- Is there anything I can celebrate or appreciate about my session?

At the end of the feedback the meeting usually ends – if there have been some issues about Safeguarding or the Ethos then sometimes it can be useful to have a short discussion of the rules or their interpretation.

Issue 2.2 Jun-2022

What are the Therapiece Nomads?

Nomads is a group for people who are looking to explore therapeutic value from a continued writing project. Whether it's a memoir, a novel, non-fiction, a songbook, or a collection of stories, whatever you'd like to explore. As Nomads, we're following an unmade path, building and gathering our projects through a series of attempts, experiments, and versions.

What makes this group different from a regular creative writing workshop is that we structure our sessions according to some therapeutic principles, including allotting equal time for each participant, practicing an author-in-charge model, and giving non-judgmental feedback (following Therapiece ethos§). Attendees who have not practiced in this way before will be guided, and we'll also learn from each other to evolve Nomads according to what we find and prefer as a group. Nomads can be seen as continuation of Therapiece - Writing in the Moment (WiM) or come from different route.

Structure still being developed

Once a month, writers will submit a piece or excerpt of up to 1,000 words. Groupmates will read and think about each other's pieces, and arrive at the session ready to make contributions or enquire.

The session will begin with an opening circle, in which each member shares what they hope to learn from the workshop, along with "what's on top" for them today, to help them clear whatever is bugging, distracting, occupying their mind.

The writer may read a passage from their work, saying what they want from the session. They will then be in charge of what themes and types of contribution which they'd like to focus on during feedback.

Workshopping will travel around the circle, with each group member having time to contribute. Once a member has spent their time, they'll be encouraged to listen – give free attention - to others' feedback in turn.

After everyone's projects have been workshopped, we'll have a closing circle, and share short reflections on how the session felt for us, whether the Ethos was followed, what came up, how feedback was received, and what might come next in our writing.

Nomads uses the same principles as WiM and Creative Writing; it's a different use of time to access a different therapeutic effect. For example, some aspects could be analogous to counselling role play. There are also possibilities for connections between pieces in a series of meetings which may have beneficial therapeutic effect. After the meeting you will receive additional contributions from the resident Nomad.

Version 2.2 Feb 2022

13

What is Therapiece Just Write?

We get together to Just Write! Generally meeting in the weeks when there are no "in the moment" meetings.

Structure is:-

    Opening circle
    Writing/Draw – four random words can be generated
    Closing circle

One thought is that Just Write provides support and reserving a place for creativity in the company of others of like mind.

Therapiece: The "Extra Pages"

Troubleshooting the processes and terms used in the Therapiece Workbook

Note on rules

We have an Ethos written down, and it is important for us to follow the kinds of values, interventions and contributions it describes, so that we are always practicing care for each other's wellbeing. However, or rather in addition, part of that care means opening and holding space for the new, the unexpected, the personal, the difficult, the raw. For that reason, and to make openness possible, we don't want to see our Ethos as a set of rules but instead as a co-created collection of guidelines and suggestions, based on our experiences.

Being non-judgemental

Expanding this phrase from our Ethos Sheet and other discussions of appropriate meeting contributions, "being non-judgemental" could mean: to accept and encourage diversity in all its forms, to be open to alternatives, whether that be alternative ways of making, talking, expressing, communicating, or belonging. In short, to not impose or expect any particular "norm" when we're entering into a Therapiece space.

Being kind and caring without comfort

One important aspect of Therapiece meetings is to let the Author talk freely. This helps them to find the most helpful expression for their thoughts, helps them not to feel judged or limited. Listeners are not there to take on the Author's difficulties but rather to give time and space to the Author, within which they can discuss any thought or feeling that comes up for them when they talk about their writing.

It is often difficult to listen without feeling the urge to comfort, but we can try to show kindness and support in other ways; simply with our presence or by saying things like "That must be hard" rather than "You are so brilliant you will get it sorted in no time."

Being self-responsible

The need to be self-responsible is a similar, but reversed, issue to the above. Just as listeners should take responsibility for not comforting or judging the Author, the Author themselves is responsible for being aware that listeners are not there to solve their issues but simply to listen and explore. The Author needs to have a level of attention that empowers them to appreciate what they are saying, take in contributions from others, and try to see them from another point of view if necessary.

Expressing concern

There may be times when someone attends a Therapiece meeting and finds that an element of the Ethos Sheet has not been followed. We want to make it possible and easy for participants to express their concern. In some situations, expressing concern won't be possible in the moment (if a judgemental or overly comforting comment is made in a session, for example, or if the breach of the Ethos occurs within an Author's time). In this case, the closing circle becomes the best place and time to express concerns from the meeting. If further discussion or clarification is needed, we can arrange as a group or involve the safeguarding team as necessary.

Listening

The listening we do in Therapiece is important. In everyday life, people often don't listen to us; they spend conversations thinking of their own responses and their own needs, or they believe they're listening well, only to quickly offer judgement or advice rather than letting the speaker continue or simply be heard. It can be distressing and triggering not being listened to.

What is involved in good listening? When we listen, we lend our resources. It is important that we hold space for the other as they explore. Being listened to might be frightening for some people, some may fear the intimacy good listening suggests. The listener should be open to this possibility.

We won't be able to predict what will be said, so all we can do is try and still our own expectations and judgements and be as open as possible to the other person. Our attention is with them, but we also need to be aware of our own reactions, so that we're not distracted by them, so we can stay "on the bank" and not be drawn into the river of their experience, to remain grounded.

Important to remember is that we can never be a perfect listener! And we don't need to understand what someone is saying in order to listen to them and hold space for them. Simply giving them the opportunity to express whatever they want can be freeing and relieving.

Contracts

A contract, often established during the Opening Circle or at the start of the Authors time, is made by the writer and presented to the group. It provides guidance on what kind of contributions and interventions the writer wants that day.
Providing a contract allows the writer to create their own boundaries, protecting themselves from unwanted kinds of feedback and maintaining autonomy. A contribution (usually called intervention in co-counselling) is an offering from another group member or reader.
An example of a contract could be: "Today I would like contributions/feedback on the emotional impact of my writing, but first I would like to explore my own feelings about the

issue I present in the piece. I would like listeners to wait until I say that I'm ready for that feedback."

Or: "Today I would like to experiment with not being asked questions. Instead I would like to simply experience free attention after I read my piece."

A "normal contract" would be a mix of free attention and one or two contributions, including statements of positive enjoyment.

One perceived benefit of these kinds of contracts is a focus on process over product/performance. They allow the reader to share and receive external input, see what emerges, be surprised, but also to be present in the moment and let go of tight control over the results of their creativity.

Version 2 Nov-2022

Differences between co-counselling and Therapiece

One aspect which is clear elsewhere in the Ethos sheet is that in Therapiece we differentiate between pieces created by a member and their own material. In Therapiece we do not comment on the person. So it is part of the way within Therapiece we encourage creativity by reflecting on the writing (art etc) and how that reaches us as listeners. Including positive comments about the writing.

There is a difficult balance here when another person piece helps to bring out some aspect for an author but generally we encourage these references if they are positive. And possibly if they give rise to some aspect for the author which they want to look at - ie not necessarily so positive but within them - within the author speaking.

Other difference between Therapiece and coco is that Therapiece aspires to use creativity to free up emotions whereas creativity is at the core of coco in the sense that the most powerful "solutions"/way forward comes from within the co-counsellor. This seems be a bit of a difference but allows each for of creativity to have benefit.

One practical difference is that in Therapiece it is accepted that the Author / speaker may wish to finish their time early. This is not often used but recognises that sometimes that creative emphasis is a bit different to a coco session. But often the author gets a new lease of speaking towards the end of their time....

Another difference is that authors are encouraged to put their piece forward if the wish to share it with others, on the Web or in the workbook.

Some coco groups do have a sense of community but this community feeling is part of Therapiece model - encouraged through the small groups (usually 4 or 5) used in meetings. If the group goes to 6 or more then it is up for discussion if the subgroups are kept constant or varied each to the group meets.

Therapiece : Optional use of the Human Givens Emotional Needs and Resources model.

One of many models for wellbeing is based on human needs. At the basic level these include Sleep, Food and Movement. Humans seem to also thrive on many complex needs and this simple tool can be used to identify in people areas which one are currently not fulfilled. The model also looks at resources which help us realise more of what we do for our wellbeing.

One view of Therapiece is that it fits in with this model – helping to provide a place to fulfil Emotional Needs and developing Emotional Resources to support this. The chart below gives some examples of this.

Theory : Toolbox talk

Communicating about how we feel is therapeutic. This includes all creative forms of communication. There is evidenced based work by Pennebaker in 1980s showing that participants who wrote about the details of "traumatic" events together with processing their feelings of events and experiences improved health and a greater sense of wellbeing. (*Health warning:* To repeatedly tell the back story is not necessarily so healthy).

Emotional Needs and *Resources*

- Attention/*Observing Self* (Author time)
- Control (Contract-Author in charge)

- Privacy <Confidential>
- Emotional Connection/*Rapport* (Sharing)
- Community (Prompts + Small Groups)
- Achievement (Feedback)
- Recognition (Co-creation>Workbook)
- Security (Induction, Safeguarding & Zoom)
- Meaning & Purpose (Expression)
- *Memory/Pattern Match (Writing from Experience)*
- *Exploring B&W Thinking (What-if)*
- *Imagination (At core of Therapiece)*

Layers of Therapiece

EN&R : When we create we feel achievement. We frame creativity in terms of emotional needs & resources. A person's emotional state needs to be given expression. If an emotional need finds its match through creativity, the pattern match can lower emotional arousal and generate new meanings and insights.

Self-exploration - Occupational – Therapeutic – Reflective 'Psychodynamic aspects (can you contradict/have you considered....?)'

Given in the Appendix are the cards used to help visualise this model for use in Therapiece and more generally.

More references can be found here:-
https://www.hgi.org.uk/human-givens
https://www.hgi.org.uk/human-givens/introduction/what-are-human-givens

and

https://www.suffolkmind.org.uk/who-we-help/mental-health-support/emotional-needs-resources/

These links are updated from time to time!

The Therapiece Safeguarding Page

You will find the **Safeguarding page here** **https://therapiece.org/members-safeguarding/**

MEMBERS SAFEGUARDING

Safeguarding

All members of Therapiece are encouraged to follow the Therapiece Ethos and use feedback within their own group to engender the mutual feeling of trust and safety in the Group and Therapiece.

If there is an occasion or series of events that any member feels that this trust is threatened or has been broken then it is their decision to use the Safeguarding process here.

As The **reporter** you need to visit this Web page Then email safeguarding@therapiece.org and-or call the number +44 1502 558373 which is an answerphone (Therapiece Safeguarding line). You should state who you are and your preferred method of initial contact with phone number if necessary. You can give as few details as you like but the date of the meeting or meetings is important.

If you have not heard back from a member of the **Safeguarding team** within three or four days you should contact the.team@therapiece and-or call +44 1502 558075 (Therapiece technical support).

The current members of the Safeguarding team are :-
Jane, Karenza, Georgina & Wakako

Therapiece Safeguarding

A simple process, resilient to human and technological error, for dealing with safeguarding is adopted at Therapiece. Here, we outline how this process should work. There are three parts to this document. Part I describes the reporting process as seen by Members of Therapiece. Part II describes the thinking behind how communication will work. Part III describes the activities of the Safeguarding Team and how the process is closed. All three parts are published and available to all members on the Therapiece Website and may be revised from time to time.

Terms

- The reporter is the person who initiates the safeguarding process.
- The object of safeguarding is the person who feels their safety is being jeopardised and is usually the same person as the reporter.
- The subject of safeguarding is the member or members who has posed the jeopardy.

NB: The reporter and object of safeguarding is generally one person. The subject of safeguarding could possibly be more than one person.

The Safeguarding team is four members of Therapiece. These roles will be reviewed annually. It is possible that the subject of safeguarding is a member of the Safeguarding team. In all cases all members will need to work together. The members of the Safeguarding team are published on the Web.

Part I: Reporting

All members of Therapiece are encouraged to follow the Therapiece Ethos and use feedback within their own group to engender the mutual feeling of trust and safety in the Group and Therapiece.

If there is an occasion or series of events in which any member feels that this trust is threatened or has been broken then they can choose to use the Safeguarding process here.

The reporter needs to visit the Web page https://therapiece.org/members-safeguarding/ then email safeguarding@therapiece.org and-or call the number +44 1502 558373

Through these channels, the reporter can describe the incident/s in their own words, in as much detail as they feel comfortable sharing and as necessary to give the team a clear sense of what has occurred.

If they have not heard back from a member of the Safeguarding team within three days, they should contact the.team@therapiece and-or call +44 1502 558075

Part II: Communication

The roles within the Safeguarding team need to be rotated and swapped if one person in the team is not available. This is an example:-

Role	Coordinator	Backup	Reserve	Resting
Period				
Q1	Jane	Karenza	Wakoko	Georgina
Q2	Karenza	Wakoko	Georgina	Jane
Q3	Wakoko	Georgina	Jane	Karenza
Q4	Georgina	Jane	Karenza	Wakoko

The reporter may wish to request a specific member of the team to handle their case.

All four members in the Safeguarding team will receive an email when a Therapiece member initiates the safeguarding process, even if the initiation was made by phone. If SG1 does not recognise the contact they will need to check if the reporter is a bona fide Therapiece member; then contact the reporter and establish the details of the events. Within 3 days SG1 will email safeguarding@therapiece.org (or call +44 1502 558373)

Part III: Progress and closure

All members of the Safeguarding team need to have each other's email and phone numbers so they can communicate with each other. At each significant step they should email safeguarding@therapiece.org to update the progress of the incident/s.

Two initial Zoom/Phone meetings need to be arranged:-

- Meeting A: With the reporter, SG1 and possibly SG2 – this is to establish details: date time people present etc.

- Meeting B: With the subject of safeguarding and SG1 and ideally SG2 as well (to observe). If there is more than one subject of safeguarding, then these will require separate meetings – i.e. not more than one subject of safeguarding in the same meeting.

A target plan needs to be established. A closure date should be mentioned in the plan. The number of meetings should be understood and possible outcomes (what each party wants) discussed. Examples of outcomes include:-

- i) The incident is recorded as closed – no details are recorded other than the name of the subject of safeguarding plus the start and end dates of the process.
- ii) The reporter or subject of safeguarding will take a break.
- iii) The reporter or subject of safeguarding will move group.
- iv) Any other resolution agreed upon that leads to closure. This may include that all parties need to focus on the Therapiece ethos, consulting others in the meeting at the time of the incident.
- v) A closure needs to be recorded but no other details than in i) above need be recorded. Closure may be recorded even if there is no resolution if the Safeguarding team agree this e.g. the recommendation is to focus on the Therapiece ethos.

All parties are encouraged to come to a conciliatory consensus.

Confidentiality needs to be observed. Each case will be different and only a broad outline of how the process should go is covered here. SG1 will liaise with the other two support members on the basis of one or two of the received emails. One or more of the Safeguarding team can discuss the issues with the reporter. Fairly early on a time frame should be agreed and maximum number of meetings established. There are a number of solutions that can be explored with the reporter — this includes practical changes, changing group, taking a break, and other resolutions may also emerge through the process. A closure needs to be recorded but no other records (start and end dates) and the name of the subject of safeguarding need be recorded.

On the issue of involving the subject of safeguarding, we can give guidance. The reporter is in charge of the decision to communicate the issue; however at the point of this being reported who is in charge shifts to the Safeguarding team. Both SG1 and SG2 need to speak to the subject of safeguarding – this can be done at the same time or at separate times. It is possible that a member of the Safeguarding team was present at the incident, but this should not affect the steps taken to resolve it.

While following these steps to close an incident, the Safeguarding team needs to be very careful to follow relevant parts of the Ethos as much as possible, including not giving advice, judging or comforting. Their role needs to ensure that those involved are heard. There can be no exclusion - except obviously a person may leave if they wish to.

NB: There is no exclusion process in place in Therapiece – this may need to change but hopefully not. A very simple exclusion process could be if the same subject of safeguarding appears in the record three times, then they are asked to leave or the current Group members of the subject of safeguarding are consulted as to whether they should be asked to leave.

Questions

Should the names of the Safeguarding team be published on the web? (Will need updating)?
Should the rota of roles of the Safeguarding team be published on the web? (Will need updating)

September 2022 version 2.3 Cocreated by Simon W and the Safeguarding team. To be adopted AGM Dec 2022

Therapiece Prompts

Introduction to the Therapiece Prompts Section

In this section of the Workbook we look at what helps with wellbeing in a creative sense. This section is a collection of prompts – exercises, idea-joggers, launchpad images – that a writer or artist can take and use to begin their own creative response. What we have found in a practical environment is that where people start from is not perhaps as significant as what they bring with them. So while the prompt has a part to play, everyone is encouraged not necessarily to use it but to write or draw what comes from within if they wish. Quite frequently even though someone might not use the prompt it is possible to see that it may have influenced the end piece.

As Therapiece is based on a peer-to-peer model it is good to take it in turns to provide a prompt but some people may feel less confident to produce a prompt so there is no pressure to do one. Rather it is worth looking at the reward of providing one – there is a sense of achievement and contributing to the group, and to the Therapiece community. These prompts tend to be timeless so a store has been built up. If you have been influenced by a prompt a year ago it can be interesting to come at it again and see if there have been changes to the way you feel about it.

It is worth using a very random prompt from time to time and this is included in these examples. It uses a random word generator on the internet which could be replaced by a preselected list of words chosen by the person providing the prompt.

Permanent prompt : Therapiece

Think of browsing or meandering somewhere – maybe all choose the same sort of place

- Boot sale
- Museum of unusual objects
- Along a river
- Through old ruins
- Or can you think of a different one?

Set the timers as usually but also add in one for 7min
When the timer goes generate a random word and try to incorporate it into you story
Set 1:30 and add three more words at 1:30 word intervals

Or write about something else!

~

This prompt stays in the Library as a current prompt and can be used if there are no other prompts or as an alternative.

Imagine a person who is opposite to you in a number of important ways. You can choose either a male or female person, but I think that this is the one aspect where you should choses the same gender as yourself not the opposite.

Make a list of say five to ten aspects – mental, emotional and physical of the biggest differences between you and the imagined person.

Write a scene where you compare how you would react and how they would react.

Or write about something else……

Writing prompt

Please suspend disbelief and in fiction or from life experience write from the point of view of an object, which either belongs to you or your protagonist.

Therapiece meeting 25-Jan-20 : Exercise, writing in the moment.

1) The quest: Think of a story, fiction or life experience, in which the characters discover something, o
   solve a puzzle or mystery, or achieve a goal.
2) Describe what the quest is for – what the main protagonists achieve or reveal.
3) Describe how the quest goes – the successes and frustrations, is it ultimately achieved or is
   something else the outcome?

Therapiece Exercise – Tuesday 23rd July 2019

Write for 15 minutes – whatever comes out after reading the following sentence, without thinking or editing.

It may be easier if you type out the sentence first, then just keep going – let your mind switch off and your imagination take over ....

"The only light in town turned on after midnight was on the back porch of the Owen's house...." *Alice Hoffman, The Rules of Magic*

Therapiece prompt 17-Aug-20

Imagine you are waiting for a friend in a café (in or out) and you can see right down the road leading to the café. You spot a person doing something unusual – what is it and why are they behaving that way. You can use the PoV of your choice or a stream of conscientious.

Therapiece prompt 25-Aug-20 Realization

Think of a day, or period, when you came to a realization – when something changed. Try to say what changed, and if you can, how and what made the realization happen. This does not need to be your own life event but can be fictional, possibly based on what happened to you.

Therapiece Prompt Mar-22 Karenza & Simon

Think about your relationship with food.

Does it help to think of the rituals associated with it? How do you prepare, cook and enjoy it? Maybe you prefer uncooked food. Who shares it with you or do you generally eat alone?

What we eat can fill us up, satisfy our cravings or leave us empty and hungry for more.

What does this bring up? Write it or about something else.....

LIFE IS A JOURNEY

SIEZE THE DAY

LOOK OUT OF EVERY WINDOW

LIVE YOUR DREAMS

DWELL IN POSSIBILITIES

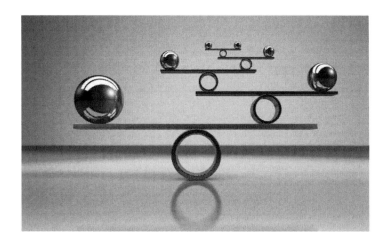

Therapiece 26-May-20 : Light at the end of the tunnel - optimism

Think of two words each - one adjective and one verb to do with something coming to an end

Free
Escape
Brave
Step-up
Release
Overwhelm

RAIN By Raymond Carver

Woke up this morning with a terrific urge to lie in bed all day

And read. Fought against it for a minute.

Then looked out the window at the rain.

And gave over. Put myself entirely

In the keep of this rainy morning.

Would I live my life over again?

Make the same unforgivable mistakes?

Yes, given half a chance, Yes.

Mystery

I truly don't know what will happen in my life, and I don't need to know. My life will unfold the way it needs to. Not needing to know keeps me open to the great mystery of life.

(Mary O'Malley)

Knowing what will happen tomorrow ruins the whole mystery of life.

(Mehmet Murat Ildan)

Anäis Nin.

Risk

And then the day came,
when the risk
to remain tight
in a bud
was more painful
than the risk
it took
to blossom.

Therapiece meeting 15-Jun-20 : Exercise, writing in the moment.

1) Think: of a story, fiction or life experience, in which the characters discover something, or solve a puzzle or mystery, or achieve a goal.
2) Write: Describe what the quest is for – what the main protagonists achieve or reveal.
3) Or Write: Describe how the quest goes – the successes and frustrations, is it ultimately achieved or is something else the outcome?

Therapiece Prompt Jeannette May-22

What comes up for you – or write about something else.

Prompt – write whatever comes up in response to this photograph.

It was an Instagram post – the author used it as a fitting end of year image.

Caroli Finch 14-Jun-22

Do not try to serve
the whole world
or do anything grandiose.
Instead, create
a clearing
in the dense forest
of your life
and wait there
patiently,
until the song
that is yours alone to sing
falls into your open cupped hands
and you recognize and greet it.
Only then will you know
how to give yourself
to the world
so worthy of
rescue.

~ Martha Postlethwaite

Writing Prompt 10-Jul-20   Walking words

You are walking - possibly on a mountain or underground, or through woods and countryside.

Just say any two words that come into your mind

Under-cliff
ooooh
cloud-bursting
rippling
Fern
Ravine
Phew
Flying

Gwyneth Hinkley
Yearning.
For what?
Past present or future.

Writing prompt 14-Jul-20

I made up a word – but what does it mean? Is it a name, is it a bird, a dragon or flagon?

Vipidiassia

Take a couple of minutes to think about what it means to you and then write it out.....
Or write about something else.....

THE ORANGE

By Wendy Cope

At lunchtime I bought a huge orange –

The size of it made us all laugh.

I peeled it and shared it with Robert and Dave –

They got quarters and I had a half.

And that orange, it made me so happy,

As ordinary things often do

Just lately. The shopping. A walk in the park.

This is peace and contentment. It's new.

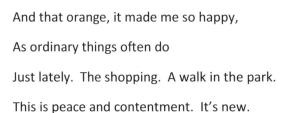

The rest of the day was quite easy.

I did all the jobs on my list

And enjoyed them and had some time over.

I love you. I'm glad I exist.

Do you believe in magic?

Write about a real life event which you experienced as magical, perhaps you were a child waking up to presents under the tree at christmas, or watching your first magic trick. Perhaps you were travelling not so long ago and saw a breathtaking view in an exotic part of the world.

Perhaps you write about it exactly as it happened, or perhaps you enhance it with some magical imagination.

Choose whichever point of view that suits you to relive the 'magical' experience.

Ring the bells that still can ring
Forget your perfect offering
There is a crack, a crack in everything
That's how the light gets in. ✨
— Leonard Cohen

Looking at character

Taken from Wonderbook by Jeff VanderMeer

WRITING CHALLENGE

This image from Shadows *by Charles Henry Bennett (London, 1850s) suggests both the hidden characteristics of a person and, perhaps, a technique: using the attributes of an animal to help in describing your character. Write a short piece describing someone you know well using only attributes of one particular animal.*

Just as the water reflects the stars and the moon, the body reflects the mind and soul.

-Rumi
muses from a mystic©

The Guest House

This being human is a guest house.
Every morning a new arrival.

A joy, a depression, a meanness,
some momentary awareness comes
as an unexpected visitor.

Welcome and entertain them all!
Even if they're a crowd of sorrows,
who violently sweep your house
empty of its furniture,
still, treat each guest honorably.
He may be clearing you out
for some new delight.

The dark thought, the shame, the malice,
meet them at the door laughing,
and invite them in.

Be grateful for whoever comes,
because each has been sent
as a guide from beyond.

by Rumi

A Fresh Start

Think about a time and possibly a place – real or imagined – where you or your protagonist has a go at a fresh start. In life, in a project, in work or relationship.

You can choose to write in any PoV, first person, second person, third person or stream of consciousness.

The other side of the fence

Think back to a situation where you struggled to see someone's point of view. Perhaps it was an argument, perhaps it was something that you did which someone reacted to in quite a strong or unexpected way. Or perhaps something they did which you reacted to in quite a strong or unexpected way. Rewrite the scenario from the other person's point of view, describing it through their eyes and trying to describe what they may have been thinking and feeling.

One Art

The art of losing isn't hard to master;
so many things seem filled with the intent
to be lost that their loss is no disaster.
Lose something every day. Accept the fluster
of lost door keys, the hour badly spent.
The art of losing isn't hard to master.
Then practice losing farther, losing faster:
places, and names, and where it was you meant
to travel. None of these will bring disaster.
I lost my mother's watch. And look! my last, or
next-to-last, of three loved houses went.
The art of losing isn't hard to master.
I lost two cities, lovely ones. And, vaster,
some realms I owned, two rivers, a continent.
I miss them, but it wasn't a disaster.
---Even losing you (the joking voice, a gesture
I love) I shan't have lied. It's evident
the art of losing's not too hard to master
though it may look like (Write it!) like disaster.

Elizabeth Bishop

MONET REFUSES THE OPERATION

Doctor, you say there are no haloes
around the streetlights in Paris
and what I see is an aberration
caused by old age, an affliction.
I tell you it has taken me all my life
to arrive at the vision of gas lamps as angels,
to soften and blur and finally banish
the edges you regret I don't see,
to learn that the line I called the horizon
does not exist and sky and water,
so long apart, are the same state of being.
Fifty-four years before I could see
Rouen cathedral is built
of parallel shafts of sun,
and now you want to restore
my youthful errors: fixed
notions of top and bottom,
the illusion of three-dimensional space,
wisteria separate
from the bridge it covers.
What can I say to convince you
the Houses of Parliament dissolve
night after night to become
the fluid dream of the Thames?
I will not return to a universe
of objects that don't know each other,
as if islands were not the lost children
of one great continent. The world
is flux, and light becomes what it touches,
becomes water, lilies on water,
above and below water,
becomes lilac and mauve and yellow
and white and cerulean lamps,
small fists passing sunlight
so quickly to one another
that it would take long, streaming hair
inside my brush to catch it.
To paint the speed of light!
Our weighted shapes, these verticals,
burn to mix with air
and change our bones, skin, clothes
to gases. Doctor,
if only you could see
how heaven pulls earth into its arms
and how infinitely the heart expands
to claim this world, blue vapor without end.

YouTube Lisel Mueller reads Monet Refuses The Operation

https://www.youtube.com/watch?v=dR1j-o_0x5A

Litany (Billy Collins)

"You are the bread and the knife,
The crystal goblet and the wine…" *- Jacques Crickillon*

You are the bread and the knife,
the crystal goblet and the wine.
You are the dew on the morning grass
and the burning wheel of the sun.
You are the white apron of the baker,
and the marsh birds suddenly in flight.

However, you are not the wind in the orchard,
the plums on the counter,
or the house of cards.
And you are certainly not the pine-scented air.
There is just no way that you are the pine scented air.

It is possible that you are the fish under the bridge,
maybe even the pigeon on the generals head,
but you are not even close
to being the field of cornflowers at dusk.

And a quick look in the mirror will show
that you are neither the boots in the corner
nor the boat asleep in its boathouse.

It might interest you to know,
speaking of the plentiful imagery of the world,
that I am the sound of rain on the roof.

I also happen to be the shooting star,
the evening paper blowing down an alley
and the basket of chestnuts on the kitchen table.

I am also the moon in the trees
and the blind woman's tea cup.
But don't worry, I'm not the bread and the knife.
You are still the bread and the knife.
You will always be the bread and the knife,
not to mention the crystal goblet and --somehow--the wine.

There is another language beyond language
another place beyond heaven and hell.
Precious gems come from another mine
the heart draws light from another source.

Rumi – Little Book of Life – from Garden of Sprit

Therapiece – what does this make you think and feel? Write about it ... or something else.

Pen Pal

Write a letter to someone or
yourself, this letter could be based
on a time in the past or the present
day. It does not have to be written
to a human, perhaps it is a body
part, an illness, perhaps it is a
personality trait or an archetype.
What would you say in this letter to
them or yourself?
Is it something that should have
been said but never was, or
something that's probably better
left unsaid but still worth expressing?

Or write

Therapiece Prompt/Exercise – Tuesday 23 March 2021

So we're going to take a few minutes to relax and go on a little journey in our imaginations before doing any writing. The writing will be what comes out from the exercise.

So, settle yourself in, and take a few deep breaths. If you feel comfortable to, close your eyes. Relax your body, and bring your attention to what is happening right now. Feel the contact of your body on what you're sitting or lying on. Listen to whatever sounds you can hear. Notice what sensations you can feel in your body. If thoughts come in just allow them to pass, there's no need to pay attention to them now, you can return to them later if you want.

And now I want you to imagine being in a safe place in nature. It might be somewhere you are already familiar with, or it could be an imaginary place. It might be by the sea, or water, in the forest, up a mountain, or perhaps even a small garden, anywhere that feels safe and welcoming. And if this is difficult for you that's absolutely fine, you can just stay with noticing what is going on in your body.

So wherever you are, listen to the sounds around you, observe your surroundings, use touch to explore different textures, and really immerse yourself in this nurturing space.

And as you explore – you might be walking, or lying on the ground, or standing looking out across the scene, you come across a building. What is it like? Large, or small? A single room or a high-rise block? Closed in or open? What's it made of?

Do you like it? What feelings come up for you? Do you want to enter it or walk round it more? Or do you want to walk away from it, or only look from a distance?

Take a few moments to explore, from outside or inside, whatever feels right and comfortable. There's no right or wrong. I'll be quiet for a few moments whilst you do this,.....

And now it's time to leave the building. You walk back through the landscape, once again noticing the sounds and the sights, the smells, the textures.

And then notice the sensations in your body as you come back to the room, to where you are sitting, to this Therapiece session. And when you are ready open your eyes....

And now you can write about what that experience was like. Either what you experienced, or the process itself. What you saw, whether that sparked any memories, gave you any insights, gave you an idea for a story, however it affected you, how you're feeling now.

Whose body ?

Somebody, **no**body **every**body

Times we might feel uncomfortable in our bodies:
- ➢ Low self esteem
- ➢ Comparing our body to someone else's
- ➢ Ate too much or need to eat something
- ➢ Illness/injury/disease
- ➢ Intense conversations or conflicts
- ➢ Situations in which we're nervous but try to come across as calm
- ➢ And many more…………..

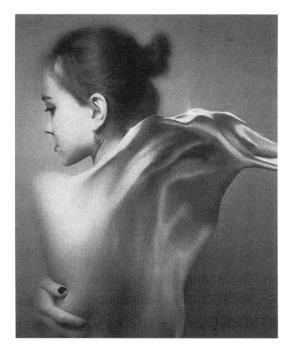

Write about a time in which you felt uncomfortable in your body, try writing at least some of it in first person and in the present tense (even if you decide to write as someone else or an animal rather than directly as yourself)

Think of an individual in a room – person or other intelligent being.

What does the room look like, and what do they look like? What are they doing and thinking? What does the room tell us about them (who may be yourself), and vice versa? All the action, if any, takes place in the room. There is no dialogue except, if you chose, internal dialogue.

If the picture below helps then please use it – if not then as you were!

Or write about something else…..

'Fire' Nikita Gill

"Remember what you must do

when they undervalue you,

when they think

your softness is your weakness,

when they treat your kindness

like it is their advantage.

You awaken

every dragon,

every wolf,

every monster

that sleeps inside of you

and you remind them

what hell looks like

when it wears the skin

of a gentle human."

May-21 Therapiece Prompt – Safety and feeling safe – being in a "safe place"

Co-created prompt – think of two or three words that you associate with being in a safe place. Then we will share and use these words as the prompt:-

Freedom

"I AM NO BIRD; AND NO NET ENSNARES ME: I AM A FREE HUMAN BEING WITH AN INDEPENDENT WILL"
CHARLOTTE BRONTE

"FOR TO BE FREE IS NOT MERELY TO CAST OFF ONE'S CHAINS, BUT TO LIVE IN A WAY THAT RESPECTS AND ENHANCES THE FREEDOM OF OTHERS"
NELSON MANDELA

Choose a way to write about the theme 'freedom'. Perhaps you will write about your perception of your own freedom, or that of others in a factual or philosophical manner. Or write a creative piece embodying or describing a character that is or isn't free.

Prompt May 24.

Imagine being a person, whom you have difficulty understanding, and maybe with whom you have difficulties.
Imagine being a person whom you would like to be.
Imagine being a person you dislike.
Imagine being an being, animal, fish, tree, plant, that interests you.
Imagine being a person with very different beliefs to your own.
Chose one, or more, or a different ? and write in the first person. I am ....
Or as usual write as the inclination takes you.

Therapiece prompt 25-May-21

You have a dream – a personal dream or a vision – describe how if feels to achieve the dream – use any PoV you like including stream of consciousness. Try to write it in the present.

If you want you can say what the dream "is" but do not feel you have to.

Or write about something else!

Therapiece Prompt 28-May-21

Write what comes to mind

If you were a place   Simon

Therapiece Prompt 9-Jun-21

If you were a place, what place would you be? You can choose a country, a town, a quiet tower or just a familiar place in your house.

Then ask yourself "how would you feel in the summer/winter?" How would you feel when you were visited by people or animals or plants…." Take a few minutes to sit with the feelings and then write.

Think about the senses

        Sight : the bright with the menacing
        Smell : the pungent with the sickly
        Touch : the rough with the slippery
        Sound : the sonorous with the rhythmic
        Taste : the salty with the aromatic

Choose a subject maybe from your opening circle or from today :-

Describe it using as many as the senses as you feel you can....

"WE ARE BORN OF LOVE; LOVE IS OUR MOTHER" RUMI

"TO DESCRIBE MY MOTHER WOULD BE TO WRITE ABOUT A HURRICANE IN ITS PERFECT POWER. OR THE CLIMBING, FALLING COLOURS OF A RAINBOW" MAYA ANGELOU

"IN A CHILD'S EYES, A MOTHER IS A GODDESS. SHE CAN BE GLORIOUS OR TERRIBLE, BENEVOLENT OR FILLED WITH WRATH, BUT SHE COMMANDS LOVE EITHER WAY. I AM CONVINCED THAT THIS IS THE GREATEST POWER IN THE UNIVERSE" N.K. JEMISIN

Use the feelings that arise from reading these quotes and any images you associate with the archetype of a mother, to inspire a piece somehow reflective of motherhood.

This could be about your mother or a mothering figure you know, your experience of being around a mother or being a mother, or simply how you experience motherhood.

(Remember we all have the capability to express mothering qualities whether we are male or female, and we do not only mother children, we can mother plants, animals, friends and family in our own ways).

Think about the past few weeks and think of a "normal or usual" day –

What part of the day did you enjoy the most?

Write what comes to mind – if you wish, you can change it to an imaginative story….

Prompt Aug-21   Gwyneth Hinkley

What does the phrase:-

        As Good As It Gets

bring up for you? Write about this or something else….

Meeting

73

Life writing or fiction : Think about a meeting – a moment in time – where you meet someone (or it could a creature – dragon, dog or dolphin). Something happens – you feel something….

What does this bring up? Write about this – or something else…

Belonging or....... ?

"Today I am taking a day off, as quiet as a feather. I hardly move though really I am travelling a terrific distance. Stillness. One of the doors into the temple"

Mary Oliver

(or write about something else)

Prompt   Gwyneth Hinkley September 2021

A watershed moment - Two sides - Heads or Tails?

<u>WiM Meeting</u>

Apparently one in three children have imaginary friends. Take some time to think about either your own childhood imaginary friends or times you played as a child at imaginary games.

What does this bring up? Write about this – or something else…

There are many ways of looking at this prompt – for example, you could create a children's story, write about connections, explore the differences in us all, be curious about the negative space and how that makes you feel etc etc.

Write/draw about what comes to mind or about something else

my brain and
heart divorced

a decade ago

over who was
to blame about
how big of a mess
I have become

eventually,
they couldn't be
in the same room
with each other

now my head and heart
share custody of me

I stay with my brain
during the week

and my heart
gets me on weekends

they never speak to one another

  - instead, they give me
the same note to pass
to each other every week

and their notes they
send to one another always
says the same thing:

"This is all your fault"

on Sundays
my heart complains
about how my
head has let me down
in the past

and on Wednesday
my head lists all
of the times my
heart has screwed
things up for me
in the future

they blame each
other for the

state of my life

there's been a lot
of yelling - and crying

so,

   lately, I've been
spending a lot of
time with my gut

who serves as my
unofficial therapist

most nights, I sneak out of the
window in my ribcage

and slide down my spine
and collapse on my
gut's plush leather chair
that's always open for me

~ and I just sit sit sit sit
until the sun comes up

last evening,
my gut asked me
if I was having a hard
time being caught
between my heart
and my head

I nodded

I said I didn't know
if I could live with
either of them anymore

"my heart is always sad about
something that happened yesterday
while my head is always worried
about something that may happen
tomorrow,"
I lamented
my gut squeezed my hand

"I just can't live with
my mistakes of the past
or my anxiety about the future,"
I sighed

my gut smiled and said:

"in that case,
you should
go stay with your
lungs for a while,"

I was confused

- the look on my face gave it away

"if you are exhausted about
your heart's obsession with
the fixed past and your mind's focus
on the uncertain future

your lungs are the perfect place for you

there is no yesterday in your lungs
there is no tomorrow there either

there is only now
there is only inhale
there is only exhale
there is only this moment

there is only breath

and in that breath
you can rest while your
heart and head work
their relationship out."

this morning,
while my brain
was busy reading
tea leaves

and while my
heart was staring
at old photographs
I packed a little
bag and walked
to the door of

my lungs

before I could even knock
she opened the door
with a smile and as
a gust of air embraced me
she said

"what took you so long?"

~ John Roedel (johnroedel.com)

80

Therapiece Prompt - Fiona Brown Dec 2021

Imagine being one of your ancestors

Where do you live, how do you live

What work do you do

What family do you have

What's your culture like

What are your main worries and hardships

What are your joys and pleasures

What is your community like

Etc.

Write a story or a reflection on one or more of any aspect that you feel drawn to with respect to your ancestry

Freedom of imagination

Suppose you have lived in a very controlling state for the past five years. All creative writing, fiction and non-fiction has been banded.

The freedom fighters break free (you might be a ringleader). It is the first day of the new spring – what would you write about? Would you look back or forward?

Of course, you have the freedom to write about something else!

"Watch carefully,
The magic that occurs,
When you give a person,
Just enough comfort,
To be themselves." ~ Atticus.

Therapiece Prompt Caroli Finch 22-Feb-22

Read the poem and then respond in any way that feels right. It may resonate with you, it may irritate you, either is perfect! See what it brings up in you, use as a jumping off point, explore how it makes you feel.

Messenger

My work is loving the world.
Here the sunflowers, there the hummingbird—
equal seekers of sweetness.
Here the quickening yeast; there the blue plums.
Here the clam deep in the speckled sand.

Are my boots old? Is my coat torn?
Am I no longer young, and still half-perfect? Let me
keep my mind on what matters,
which is my work,

which is mostly standing still and learning to be
astonished.
The phoebe, the delphinium.
The sheep in the pasture, and the pasture.
Which is mostly rejoicing, since all the ingredients are here,

which is gratitude, to be given a mind and a heart
and these body-clothes,
a mouth with which to give shouts of joy
to the moth and the wren, to the sleepy dug-up clam,
telling them all, over and over, how it is
that we live forever.

Mary Oliver

2022-02-28 Fiona Jamieson - Mrs Winchester outlet

Write what come up – or something else

The Therapiece Pieces

Introduction to the Therapiece Pieces Section

Very simply here are some examples of pieces written or created in Therapiece meetings. The method of selection was random based on members' willingness to share them. The idea behind this section is to show the variety of the pieces and give confidence to others who would like to join in.

Do I believe in magic?

When I was a child life seemed to be made of magic. Everywhere I was taken was 'child friendly' there would be toys to play with, children to play alongside, I could sit in the trolley at the supermarket, and at the end my parents would use paper and plastic to take it away with them, and I would stare longingly at the cashier, who from my perspective had been given the very special job of scanning each product. Life was a breeze, if I needed to get somewhere on time, which let's be honest consisted of the least serious things, like other children's birthday parties and playdates, I would somehow arrive there, on time, without any effort on my part. And when it was time to go home again, I would magically be transported home and fed. Every evening would be full of books containing even more magical realms of mystery and beauty. I guess it's safe to conclude that a supportive, loving and safe childhood is in some sense a magical experience.

Of course, now I am old enough to understand that there is always an underlying explanation to any magic trick. I know I have people to thank. And that before anything in life is understood, it will always contain an essence of mystery about it. I suppose the more we know the less magic there is. Although there is some magic that cannot be taken away, like the magic moments of emotion and feeling. These days 'magical' emotions and feelings are usually catalysed by nature, in the form of spectacular views, animals investigating the world, babies clutching their tiny fists around your finger and staring at you through a set of wide and unassuming eyes. So I suppose it's also fair to conclude that an adult's life lived in nature, or at least with the capacity to notice nature, can be in some sense a pretty magical experience.

In short, yes, I do believe, I might just believe in magic.

Piece : Children

I always wanted a child, or did I? I wanted first to be a social worker and presumed I'd be a mother. My child was an accident. I was 35. I never considered abortion, but did think if it was too difficult I could have her, or one of them (twins) adopted. That sort of says to me as I write it, how little I bonded with the babyinthewomb. I remember sitting on a speaker at a party and a friend's husband telling me off. I remember way into the pregnancy a friend being anxious because I couldn't feel the movement of the baby. I wasn't anxious at all. I remember during the birth eventually accepting gas and air, coming back to consciousness, and it felt such a long long time. I said the baby's dead isn't it, oh well I don't mind too much. As I write all this speaks to me of ambivalence.

After the birth I remember lying on a bed, the baby in a cot beside me, both awake, and just looking at each other. They gave me a needle to put me to sleep. Until now I'd felt angry with the needle people, but in this moment I feel profound gratitude for being given that moment, and all the work they did over 15 (17) hours of induced labour to bring my baby safely safely into the world. She is called Beckie. She is now 43. She wrote a poem to me,

When she was tiny and we were still in hospital, she didn't put on weight. They said she wasn't getting any milk from me, but I knew she was, because she wasn't daft, and she wouldn't suck for no reason. They insisted on a bottle, I gave her as much as she wanted, and then lied about her having finished it all. My very dear friend, Joyce, said I was a very poor liar.

Somewhere I have the story of her birth. I couldn't sleep for many nights after the birth, and a friend suggested I wrote down what I remembered. I must find and read it. It was a very difficult birth.

As I sit now I think that something in me maybe died in the years after her birth. Colin's betrayal, Tom dying, Chris killing herself, Charles' interest coupled with his distancing, the loss of my communal living, so many many blows. My parents were great, me an unmarried mother albeit 300 miles away, and even my mother coming up trumps..

Karenza-Monica Case - 20-Feb-20

Prompt about archetypes – Creator/Artist.

When the urge to create visits it's almost impossible to ignore. The feeling of restlessness, of excitement, of something bigger and more expansive that wants to emerge is too strong to dismiss or disallow. And until the work is fully expressed in form it continually needles and points towards and suggests. There is no rest until it has been shown the light, until the creator is spent.

How does one quantify a value, let alone an enduring one? The originating idea, once expressed, and exposed, falls back into the ethers from whence it came, no longer a driving force, a catalyst which has done its job. The value is in the process, the expression, the time it was being created. It may have value to the receiver, creating an impact. It may move some or disturb others.

For some there be a vision, to make visible or audible or tangible, to create in reality a concept or an idea. But for others the act itself is the creation - the making of marks, the writing of words, the voicing of sounds, are art in themselves. Transient, temporary, on their way to a continual evolving into something deeper, or different.

An archetype can only be general, generic. I wonder whether the creator of archetypes is influenced by his own archetype, and may therefore be unable to fully and objectively describe what may not be one he or she embodies.

CF

Piece : Getting Old

Growing old, body not working as well, no longer being a sex object, (thank heaven, feeling so much freer and less under threat in the world). Having to say goodbye, say goodbye to people as they die, having to say goodbye to yesterday, knowing that it won't come back. Not only that yesterday can't be reproduced, but that the activities of yesterday are now beyond me, or at least much more dangerous to a frailer, more brittle body.

Brittle, there's an interesting word, it rather well describes this body with-it's fungussy toe nails, broken finger nails, and bones that shout we can't afford to fall down.

Growing old, wrinkly skin, past it, no longer relevant to anybody. Loved yes, but in a sort of, 'Oh is she still here sort of way.'

Purpose, raison d'être. I volunteer with refugees to pay my entitlement to continue to breathe the air, and in order to have useful connection with someone, to be of service to someone.

Death. What does death look like? A passing, a letting go, an end to this suffering, a no more place, a rest, I want my daughter and granddaughter to have warning, to not be shocked, but I don't want a lengthy drawn out process.

I believe that a peaceful birth and a peaceful death are important to the universe, because they are pivotal moments of energy. And not only human births and deaths, all births and deaths. The destruction of healthy trees is an affront, a traumatising of nature. If I die in pain, unable to breathe, desperate and despairing, that puts a traumatising energy into the world, which It can certainly do without.

All I know, all I've learned. All that will disappear when I die, along with my pension!

I grieve the passing of all I've learnt, the way from A to B over the Pyrenees, as well as all my learnings, all will die with me. I guess that's why people write books.......Maybe it's not just a form of narcissistic self indulgence.

Do I hear the note of envy in my voice?

Karenza-Monica Case – 20-Feb-02

She was sitting waiting for her friend. There was a lot of activity going on in the small café, people chatting and laughing, the clink of cutlery and chairs being pushed back against the floor. The coffee machine, in full view, was creating more noise and a lot of steam.

Susan sat by the open door. She chose this position so that she could look down the street to see when her friend John arrived. She always liked to arrive early so she could settle in and orient herself.

She also liked to people-watch and people-listen. Sometimes her imagination would run wild after hearing snippets of conversation, and she would suddenly find herself transported into other worlds, worlds of fantasy and illusion, worlds that she never thought she could inhabit except in her dreams.

To the outside world they may not have appeared to be very adventurous or exciting, but to Susan they were a far cry from the rather reserved life that she led.

Today was no different. Peering down the street she witnessed a performer standing outside another shop. Dressed as a clown, with large floppy shoes and with white make-up contrasting against a big red smile, he was making large gestures with his whole body.

Turning his head from side to side, making big staring stances, and saying absolutely nothing, it felt quite creepy to Susan.

After a few moments of watching, she found herself enter another world, an alien environment a bit like a fairground, with old fashioned merry-go-rounds, hoopla stalls and candy floss kiosks. Scattered between these were little mini-theatres where puppets and toys without operators were enacting various events.

They were accompanied by a cacophony of sounds – bells, and drums, strange sounding whistles, and music that she'd never heard before.

It was bedlam. Susan was surrounded by visual imagery, immersed in noise, mesmerised by the activity.

She then made an enormous decision – she decided to join in....

CF

There is another language beyond language
another place beyond heaven and hell.
Precious gems come from another mine
the heart draws light from another source.

Rumi – Little Book of Life – from Garden of Spirit

another mine another yours
my language not yours
is that the trouble
I feel your meaning
I think mine

some many gems are from you
that remain uncut in mine
shouting quietly
for attention
what language is understood

what is just guessed at
or at least lines undisturbed
least it should frighten me
turned like a spirit in a grave
what language is like torque

ah that brings me to a place
beyond hell and heaven
a haven of incessant concept
conveyed by phonemes of thought
what is language if it is not the conveyor

thoughts and feelings hidden within me
somehow struggling out to slay ennui
how come I'm last to know what I'm seeking
little marks of mine seeking gems
rolling by watching thoughts

is there a membrane so thin between
what I think and what I feel
is there a language where they are the same
where I can think love
and feel thoughts

Part of the Day

We load the rucksack, 2 folding chairs and 2 shopping bags into the boot of my car.

Off we go on the short trip to some off-road parking. We walk along a path between nettles into a small old wood, set on a steep slope. We must tread carefully between tree roots and down a few wooden steps, helpfully placed by the Council.

Already the scene is inviting us in. it's quiet, except for the sounds of nature. And the smell of the river. There's lots of shade provided by the large old trees which have both seen so much and hold the space with such reverence.

We arrive full of excitement and anticipation and not giving our attention to the trees at all!

Firstly, we set up a chair each with our respective bags holding our towels, flasks, and other paraphernalia to make our ending more comfortable.

Next the rucksack needs to be unpacked. The deflated paddle board is laid out like a shroud!

With many occasions of getting it wrong we now know how to blow it up without losing air. It's a lot of effort but I'm usually spared this task on account of my age and my back. Next, the fin has to be forced into position. We have a rubber mallet to help with this.

With our costumes under our clothes, we're ready in a jiffy.

Up the river we go. One of us swimming and the other on the PB.

Now we focus on our surroundings. They draw us in.

All chatter dissipates and we just know each other is there.

The gentle sounds of the movement of the water caresses our ears.

The sounds of birds' overhead, both near and far.

The open fields arising and passing.

Great big overhanging trees to navigate.

A field of cows curiously watching our progress.

A swan who's a bit spooked by our presence and doesn't know what to do.

This has been my favourite time, Sunday, and Monday mornings with my daughter for several weeks now.

Piece : A positive place

I'm in my grandma's back room. I've just come home from school. My Mum is in hospital. My little brother is having a nap in his pram. My little sister is here, but I'm going to pretend she isn't, because I never know what to do about her. That's another story. It's summer. My grandma has given me a biscuit. My grandad will be home from work soon, he always smells so lovely snuff and machine oil. The top of the buses also smells like that. I love him. I love his grumpiness. He is real. My grandma is so sweet to us, but you never quite know....... I've never heard a cross word from her though. She gives us a spoonful of condensed milk sometimes, but not before meal times. Their front room used to be a shop. It is warm. It is safe. I feel safe. I don't have to be on my guard for the unexpected. My grandma likes touching us. Being with her is so simple. She knows she is the grown up. My grandad also. He is crotchety, but he never wants to hurt me. This is a healing time. I feel my bits, not blown apart, but fragmented, because usually it's safer that way. They are knitting together. I feel myself becoming whole in this place of healing. My grandma is going to join me into the library. The library is between this home and my parents' house. I will be able to go, just like a big girl, when I go back to my parents. They all say that will happen when my Mum is better. Maybe she won't get better. I feel so awful when I say that. That is a real sin. You have to honour your Mum and Dad. Especially your Mum, she is a woman and has done a big thing she has given me life. I am glad for my life, but I am not glad for her, she is too complicated, and she doesn't know she is supposed to be the grownup.
So back to this room. There is a rag rug in front of the fireplace. That is the sort of rug you make with pieces of material and a big needle. It's got a funny rough texture. I think grandma made it. She says she will teach me to knit. I love her. And I love my grandad. And I love my brother. I feel so bad I can't say I love my little sister, but she is so empty, and complicated, I draw back. I'm afraid of getting lost in her. I've learnt not to go near my Mum, because I can be lost in her. But it doesn't seem fair not to go near my little sister.

Karenza-Monica Case – 20-Feb-21

Secret Shame
(What I really Want you To Know)

A thief from six. New caps
for my gun. The telephone money for
trillions of sweets
that were never enough.
And later still, false fur, a tail
for Basil Brush,
soft toys for my heart.

A house surrendered
and not the first.
Life stealing back.

Bankrupt twice, and heading for third,
not got what it takes.
Ill and no use, unlucky I think,
My, do I try, yet a victim still.

I say 'no bother', but can't be
bothered. Can't care to care,
unless I can, sometimes.

Dishes left for days,
pans piled high, surfaces
unwashed. Like me.
One year, three jumpers,
what to wear too much.

A lump of snot on my sleeve
from an earlier sneeze.
Gross. And intriguing.

Can't stop eating,
wanting.
Shaming,
numbing,
stuffing down,
postponing pain.

Drops of rain slide down a
different pane.
I am a child again. The blackbird
croaks, I forget it all.
This moment - everything.

I write.
I smile.
I talk to plants.

Oh subtle shame,
oh seductive shame,
you think your words and labels
can keep me captive.

But now I see...
you are *not* the facts.

Secrecy is your substance,
you shrivel in the Light.

You continue to imprison until
my words are met, but it's
only a matter of time...
The secret's out ..
And I am free.

Caroli

Prompt: If you were a place, what place would you be? You can choose a country, a town, a quiet tower or just a familiar place in your house.

I'm the tip of a spire on the tallest church in town – I can see the coming and goings in the market square and have done for centuries. Occasionally a pigeon or other bird (than goodness we don't have seagulls and that cows don't fly) comes and sits on me but generally I have a fantastic view all around. I don't really have a favourite time of year or day but I guess I would have if I was human, animal or bird.

I love to see the people coming and going, I notice when there are plagues and wars this changes for a time – the market square is empty for a while. I can't effect things but can see much - far and wide. I see no difference between good and evil – no difference between fine and bad. "What is" happens and "what is not" is only in my imagination.

I see the joy of the people as they dance and make merry – I see the sorrow and the pain as their fight for life but are defeated by death and disease – famine and other unnatural events, like social media.

But I see each generation start afresh – beginning again with a fresh slate – a clean sheet – built-in forgiveness – perhaps only to be influenced by the past but also aspire opportunity for the future.

Some call it progress, others Armageddon – but from up here it looks like life.

The Moving Finger

It was the day   before his sixtieth birthday.   Next week there would be no more office to go to, he was now officially retired.

He had given his working lifetime to the bank.   Started straight from school, was diligent, impressed his superiors, took every opportunity for enhancing his qualifications.   He advanced: chief cashier, under manager   then manager of the branch   where he had started out.

There had been the opportunity to work in the large city office which he took and for a while, commuted daily into town.   However , his wife (they had met at the local club where they had played tennis as teenagers) was unhappy about the long evenings she spent alone when he was travelling back from the city.   He asked to be transferred back to his local branch.

He led an ordered life, lived in a tidy home with a careful wife who looked after him with predictable efficiency.   They no longer played tennis but walked their dog along the towpath of the canal.

He would appear to be a contented, successful man who lived a predictable life with annual holidays, the odd cruise and city visits but mainly they liked the little Devon hotel they had once stayed in and repeated the experience often.

Tomorrow would be different.   His life was to be punctuated by a change.   An enormous change.

He had an airline ticket secreted in his pocket, a new suitcase packed with new lightweight clothes.   He had left it at the Left Luggage office.

Tomorrow he planned to escape from his defined life, far away.   Perhaps he would paint and enjoy an existence so different from his chronicled life.

Men and my power. I've two guys staying with me at the moment. They're nice guys but..... they don't see. So the washing goes out but no sense of it needing to come back in, jobs are half done, no sense of a tidy completion.

How do they live? Is it just that, in the presence of a woman, the undone will of course get done. Stuff that for week of Sundays.

So I have to tell them what to do? I feel unpleasant doing that. I like to be alongside people. Telling people creates a division?

When tell these two they are very willing!

My power? A guy once said that I ate men for breakfast! I didn't recognise this person. My sense of me was that if you stood up to me, I'd just back down.

So what is my history with men.... an absent father, war time, guys in planes bombing me, my Mum and my little sister. Men making war, men ruling the world. Male energy feeling entitled, born with that male silver spoon in their mouth. Male priests who disregarded anything difficult.

A grandfather who still looks after me, a father doing his very best, a first boyfriend who just stopped writing after two years.

M'y feeling let down when I think of me. Let down by a father who didn't protect me from my Mum's daftnesses. Let down by a first love in whom I'd places all my trust. Let down by a series of politicians. Let down by bosses who didn't see the bigger picture. Let down by the general idiocy of so many men, the narrowness of their vision. My let down feels very powerful.

And yet men, in their simplicity are easier than women in their complexity.

Let down by men, who promise so much, and give so little. Let down by a very male God who was not there when I needed him a child.

And yet I've survived! I'm a winner, I'm a winner in part as a result of my own actions, but far more than that, as a result of the gifts life has offered me.

It's the presumption men have. I'm a man and so...... The Boris Johnstoness of so many of them. And why do we women not claim our world, our power? From whence my reluctance to boss the two guys around? From whence my reluctance to ..... is it that we hate the men power so much that we won't claim our share of it.

I think of Greek and Roman times, their Goddesses, and maybe their power was held in sneakiness, rather than up front challenge.

Setting : In the future when the Mars virus hits mother earth. A small consulting room in a secure mental hospital.

The second time I met my psychiatrist he looked at me - small round glasses glinting he opens with:-

Him: So you think that the world was manipulated in to a mass inoculation do you?
> Me: Not really – I suppose more a case of mass fear – it had quite a lot of good outcomes – helped reduce carbon foot print etc etc – no I'm more concerned that how accepting or unquestioning everyone has been.

Him: Does that explain why you were sectioned – for being subversive?
> Me: Oh no, that that was quite understandable – I have a long history of mental health and I fully recognise that I was sectioned for my own and others safety – my family and so on.

Him: Do you expect me just to discharge you as you are obviously completely sane?
> Me: No not at all – I find it very interesting talking to you and would not wish you to discharge me until you're absolutely certain that I am "normal".

Him: What do you think normal is?
> Me: It is easier to say what it is not – I worked as a statistician in a small group of about 8 statisticians - all eccentric except one who seemed normal – so that made him a misfit. I suppose the best definition is someone who can live their life without being hospitalised in a mental health hospital. Would you say?

Him: What would you say? – I was taught to say this is about you not me.
> Me: Are you so sure? Can you envisage this discussion is about you?

Him: It does not matter what I think, this is about you.
> Me: In that case yes then I do wonder if the world was manipulated in to mass inoculation. That makes me feel more normal.

Him: Would you say that there was a conspiracy, for some ulterior motive, the masses where manipulated into all going for a vaccine?
> Me: I believe the world was manipulated in to mass inoculation. I'm not sure I would call it a conspiracy – rather closer to home – I might describe it as a mass gaslighting.

Him: Have you experienced gaslighting?
> Me: I have never experienced an attempt to gaslight me.

His eyes glinted double time during a pause
Him: But you had the vaccine…. Do you feel that through your actions or inaction you managed to gaslight the population of earth in to mass inoculation?
> Me: *No answer – silently looking at him*

Him: I will see you again in a week.

I am Israel. I am surrounded by what doesn't like me. I'm not unhappy about this. In fact I'm used to it. It's my norm. I never ask myself why? What would be the point, whatever I do they don't like me, and they never have. I can tell you this, but don't tell the others, there are people in my country, who disagree. They say that's it is not inevitable, that it happens because of what I do. However I shut them up, by pointing to the fact that my neighbours declared war on me as soon as I was born, and then again in 1967.
I'm doing a real good job now however. I'm getting bigger and bigger, OK, it's not solid territory, it has odd specks of country that I don't fully control, but they get less and less. Some less than friendly people call it Zionisn, or even Colonialism. ME I know it's just taking back what belonged to me, albeit so long ago.
I've a very disparate set of inhabitants. They can hardly agree on anything. It's a good job, that I can keep them thinking they are under threat. In that way, they stay united aginst the common enemy. In fact when I look back to before I had Israel, I guess that was part of what made jewishness survive. Given all the threat from the outside world we had to hold together.
I wonder what creature I would be, Ahh yes a spider, sending out my tentacles of possession, sending out my tentacles of influence, sending out those that create friction, that turn neighbour on neighbour, that escalate wars. Do you know I destroyed the to be Prime Minister of the UK with my………Anti semetic label. That one is very useful.

Me I am Palestine. What creature would I be. I'd be a oyster, that spider across the way may send out his tentacles, he may cut every village and town from contact with its neighbour bur he'll never destroy the kernel of what it is to be Palestinian. I also know that when right is one's side one will win through. Evil and aggression has its victories, but it never wins the day.

I am an Israeli, I am 17 years old. I don't know what to think. I don't know what to believe, I feel pulled and torn from one side to the other. My heart tells me that it is wrong to cause misery. My heart echoes with the hurt it sees my country do. And I want to survive. How can I stand out against the will of Israel and belong in Israel. The only way to be different here is to face ostracisation, to face those that remind you of the holocaust, remind me of my great grand parents who almost died in the camp, of my young aunts who did die. If I sympathise with suffering of the, the Arabs , then they point to our suffering.
I hate to live in this fear, not knowing where the danger comes from? Is it from across the border or from within?

Expletive embroidery

- Oh blast and damnation
- I think you will find you mean fuck and shit
- Well at least you stop at the c-word
- You mean "see you next Tuesday"?
- Yes precisely – at that point the profanity dilutes the effectiveness.
- Says who – who the fuck says?
- Do you remember Billy Connolly talking about "fuck", how you cannot use it gently as in "fuck off he hinted"?
- Yes I remember now just get on with your fucking embroidery and stop side tracking.
- And Monty Python got round it with silly bunt – from a man who could not say the letter c. Still you can spell it with a k.
- Have you noticed that mostly the less extreme expletives are to with bodily functions or male organs but it is the female one that is considered the worst?
- No I haven't – and you're a right tit.
- I suppose there is that one …. But plonker, dick, dick head, cock…. are in the majority.
- Yes hen – you've dropped a stich there.
- I suppose penis is not really a term of abuse.
- It is a joke though.
- Then there is D H Lawrence who (very serious) in his introduction to Lady Chatterley noticed someone he met was obsessed with the f-word covering his entire day with it describing it at all until he got home and then discovered his wife having sexual intercourse with the priest.

Anon Feb 2022

Theme: Calmness: Brain storming words: excited storm, parts, pockets, private, serene, siren, story

Here is my story on 9th Aug 21 with the above words:

There is an eerie calmness about the sea. So still and serene. The mottled sky is reflected in the calm, and it casts shadows and hues across the ocean. It feels like I'm being held in my own private embrace by the grandeur of it all.

Until, up from the sea arises the Leviathan, it's back breaching first then a spout of water reaching several meters high. What a sight.

The ocean is excited to the level of a storm. It's become awesome in its size and effect.

Part of me is gobsmacked and frozen to the spot on which I stand. Another part is wondering if I should run away to safety. Instead, I slowly lift my hands and tuck them into my pockets for safe keeping. That seems enough. I don't want to miss a thing.

My eyes stay focused on the beast while my senses roam around the outer edges of the scene, determined to drink it all in; allowing myself to become intoxicated.

I'm so absorbed that I find myself shocked to the core when the siren goes off, alerting the coast guard to the incident. It shakes me out of my reverie. I'm back in the real world again.

What a shame!

Looking through the window Heart sighed at what she witnessed – leaves on the trees fluttering in the slight breeze, the chirruping of long-tailed tits as they landed and took off from the branches, a slight misty early morning haze highlighting the first rays of the sun. Heart felt happy.

Head found itself counting the number of birds, then commenting on the murky weather outside. Soon it was complaining that it was a work day, which meant tedious, pointless tasks on the computer. Before long it was wondering what the point of life was, a helpless victim feeling powerless to change anything.

Heart saw Head's descent into misery and was sad. Although unable to help directly it made an appeal to the lungs who agreed to step in. Heart asked Head to join with it and with lungs.

With both of their attention on the rhythmic inhale and exhale of the diaphragm, the air passing in and out, Head and Heart found themselves relaxing and enjoying a peaceful state of no-thing-ness. An eternal spaciousness which neither judged nor interpreted, but which simply existed as itself. A beautiful fullness, lacking nothing. Ever present, in total alignment with the cosmos.

I'm married to John, I've 4 daughters and no son. That's not an easy thing because John has a farm, and farms need sons. It's wartime. There are bombs falling on my nearest city, Coventry. I don't think I've ever been there. We go places in a pony and trap, and it's too far. We go to Kenilworth to church etc.

Margaret, Mary and Monica live on the farm with John and I. But Teresa has married, she married Harold, his father works as a toolmaker. Harold's a bit above that, but not much. He's an insurance agent.

As I Karenza, named Monica at birth, write this, I feel ashamed at how little I know, how little interest I've had in my family. Ashamed also at my dismissal of Grandma Wood, and her coldness to us, her criticisms of me.

Who was she? 4 daughters. I've been given a copy of the family history by my sister in law.

What am I doing with my life that I have so little interest in looking back? What is and from where comes my feeling. Lowness. I think there is shame.

John makes me do things I don't like. I don't know if they're normal things.

Now I am old I dress all in black. I'm sort of round. My hair is very white. I wear lots of layers. I feel so powerless, and yet I'm quite a tyrant. Nothing, nothing, nothing, never ever will ever satisfy me. They will never be good enough. They will always fail. I'm angry because maybe Teresa in escaping, in marrying will be good enough. Maybe she'll succeed where I've failed. I can't stand that. I have to stop that. I have to destroy joy.

Why, why why my granddaughter asks before she dies. A flame has to be put out. My flame was put out, so all the flames have to be put out.

What is needed to heal this? Warmth and forgiveness. Each of us does our best, in our very different, disturbed, troubled, and sometimes even criminal selves.

Karenza-Monica

"Ring the bells that still can ring
Forget the perfect offering.
There is a crack, a crack in everything.
That's how the light gets in."

Leonard Cohen.

The picture is of a statue with a cloud going through it. So the evening sunset cloud is going through the statue. I like the Leonard Cohen song that goes with the picture.

I heard him performing the song on TV once. It's good, because it's saying imperfect is good. Imperfect is actually the correct answer. A plea against perfectionism. Perfectionism is a dark, stagnant, dead place. Imperfection is light and life. That is a nice thought, a hopeful thought. As perfectionism is impossible to achieve anyway. It lets us all off the hook. It's life affirming.

It's about old age too. "The bells that still can ring." Do what you still can do. It won't be as much as before, as perfect, as fast, as well done, as well remembered as before – but that's how the light gets in.

So presumably, when we're dead, the crack has just broken completely open, and that's when we see nothing BUT the light, when we cross to the other side – often it's a bright light that people see. That is the light getting in, but strangely, when we are dead and gone.

Jane Taylor

The gut feeling.

I have just consumed 2 Finest tuna and St Ayure pitta breads. And now my gut is thinking.

I am understanding that the gut is the second brain. Which I expect is why one has "gut feelings". The stronger the gut feeling the more one might be inclined to act.

Actions when accompanied by words

are more important than words
without actions.

The most important combination
of words and actions are those
that match so the action actually
follows the words like a form
of truth.

Of course the brain in one's gut
is connected to the mind in the
primary brain. Some times the
two brains are syncronized and at

other times the brains do not work together. It is odd because one should always do what one's gut suggests, as opposed to what one's mind suggests because the latter can sometimes trick a person. The gut rarely if ever lies though.

Thoughts embeded in food

20/8/21 Continuation in Just write

If one considers that as one prepares food and thinks about the day and

There is a Spanish film called
"Like water for chocolate." that is
a translation of the spanish title.
The woman, a chef, in this film puts
such love into the preparation that
the consumers of her food do loving
acts after eating her fare.

It is reminiscent of the song
Wine, woman and song, by either
Whitesnake or Free.

The gut therefore records and
plays back truthfully the consumed
food. Whereas the mind would
lie & deceive at certain times

perhaps the gut is there to
tell the mind to employ
caution. The mind I would
expect to remember longer that
the memory of the gut. The gut
would tell a person to do something
almost immediately, whereas with
the mind you might make &
execute a plan.
The plan is refined by the gut on
a more short-term basis.
So the Gut vs The Mind is a
symbiotic relationship.

Therapiece 22.09.2020 David Robertson

The Time Traveler and the Gypsy

The time traveler looked a the Gypsy's rather unkempt atire with a certain mistrust.

The Gypsy looked back at the time traveler with a mutually distrustful regard, despite the casual look of the fellow.

The Gypsy had spent the night under the hedge. Sleeping rough was part of their life and made for the character that they were.

In comparison the time traveler looked a bit frazelled as if he had consumed a bit too much LSD. In fact they were on dopamine ordering anti psychotics which stabilized them enough to carry on as normal after travelling backwards and forwards to find what was going to happen and to find out how what had happened had happened. The effects of time travel stretched the mind something cruel, although the benefits of the information gathered were quite impressive.

The Gypsy had in fact consumed some LSD two nights before, which is how they happened to be under the hedge the night before. They had had to dance the first night round a big open fire that their friends lit to celebrate the betrothal of a cousin or two. The fact that the betrothal had happened months before had nothing to do with the fact that they still celebrated it.

The Gypsy asked the time traveler, "Tomorrow? How far is that?". The time traveler said, "Our tomorrow, is the same number of hours as today was yesterday away from today."

Gypsy asked another question, not looking too baffled by the previous answer. "OK, What if I told you I want eggs for breakfast tomorrow, beans for lunch and sausages for dinner? Will my want be satisfied, or do I die tonight and never know tomorrow as you do?".

The time traveler said, "I am not going to answer that question. I shall refer you to a friend of mine." He pointed across the road and there was an undertaker. Check with Billy Bob McTaverty. He shall help you find the answer.

All...

David

The time traveller and the Gypsy

The Time Traveller and The Gypsy

The time traveler looked at the Gypsy's rather unkempt attire with a certain mistrust.

The Gypsy looked back at the time traveler with a mutually distrustful regard, despite the casual look of the fellow.

The Gypsy had spent the night under the hedge. Sleeping rough was part of their life and made for the character that they were.

In comparison the time traveler looked a bit frazzled as if he had consumed a bit too much LSD. In fact, he was on dopamine ordering anti psychotics which stabilized them enough to carry on as normal after travelling backwards and forwards to find what was going to happen and to find out how what had happened had happened. The effects of time travel stretched the mind something cruel, although the benefits of the information gathered were quite worthy of the side effects. To travel in time to visit the future and the past was a feat not for the faint hearted. The time traveler was brave to move in time not entirely knowing if he would or could return to the present and continue his life. However, time travel was necessary in order to continue the present. All manner of amazing feats were called for in the survival of humans.

The fact that the time traveler had to consume anti-psychotics to remain free in the present was simply a by-product of his occupation. One would think he would stop traveling in time so that he could come off the medication, however, it was not as simple as that. The urgency within him was a part of his mindset that sensed trouble in the future and his need to abate that trouble to prevent a disaster so that life would not be extinguished on Earth before it completed its reason for being.

Many sought the answer to the reason for the Earth human's existence, and Time travelers tended to know what that reason was intuitively. They simply were not allowed to express it for the knowledge should not be communicated to a non-time traveling being.

The Gypsy had in fact consumed some LSD two nights before, which is how he happened to be under the hedge the night before. They had had to dance the first night round a big open fire that their friends lit to celebrate the betrothal of a cousin or two. The fact that the betrothal had happened months before had nothing to do with the fact that they still celebrated it.

The life of a Gypsy was not as free as it might seem, they had to negotiate entrance to town and village as people were automatically suspicious of their ilk. The suspicion was often misguided as they only usually caused trouble to cause a solution to occur for their family or wider community. There was a coincidental disappearance of items from property within the vicinity of a Gypsy encampment. The Gypsy would explain that local criminals pinched items when Gypsy's were in the area and frame them, so they get the blame. Of course, the local criminals would simply smile and ignore the aspersion casting.

The time traveler knew this to be the case as he consumed thought of the future where he might help his conversationalist. Soon the time traveller had the picture and planned a diplomatic end to the meeting.

The time traveler sensed the coming dialogue and knew that what he was about to say would not give him much sleep tonight, another side effect of time travel. He always thought that it was worth it. One thing he missed though were surprises. He would really like something to happen which was a surprise. Or would he. Would he be able to cope with a violent surprise? He normally managed to leave a situation before it manifested into physical violence as he sensed through the time matrix, an urgency to vacate the area.

So, the meeting of the Gypsy and the Time Traveler was an amicable one, without judgement and without friction. The parting was a bit strange though and came about in the way documented below.

The Gypsy asked the time traveler, "Tomorrow? How far is that?". The time traveler said, "Our tomorrow, is the same number of hours as today was yesterday away from today."

Gypsy asked another question, not looking too baffled by the previous answer. "OK, what if I told you I want eggs for breakfast tomorrow, beans for lunch and sausages for dinner? Will my want be satisfied, or do I die tonight and never know tomorrow as you do?".

The time traveler said, "I am not going to answer that question. I shall refer you to a friend of mine." He pointed across the road and there was an undertaker. "Check with Billy Bob McTaverty. He shall help you find the answer."

Therapiece Testimonials

Here are some Therapiece Testimonials.

Sue: Did my first session on Therapiece …really really good. Surprised me as I wouldn't say I'm a writer. To give myself writing space gave me freedom to explore…a feeling if connection & joy.

I'm doing a monthly Zoom Therapeice Group. Thank you Therapiece for this inspired concept and for making it happen. 29-Jan-20

Carol: Whether I follow the prompts, write stream of consciousness, or describe what's on my mind, what I love most about Therapiece sessions is that I always *feel* different afterwards – lighter, less burdened, just changed in some way, as if I've let go of something.

When I start writing, I usually have no idea of what will emerge, and am often surprised at what comes out, material that I can reflect on later in my own time and perhaps explore further.

Everyone brings, and takes, different things from Therapiece. For me the process is more important than what I produce, because it seems to bypass my mind and accesses a place that seems more authentic and heartfelt, and which tends to get overlooked in the course of daily life.

Expressing how I feel, and being heard, in a safe environment, has boosted my self confidence, and attending regularly has increased my imagination and creativity. 3-Mar-20

David: Therapiece came along and did not fill a void, it did not hurt me, it did not do my head in. It opened a moment, it crossed a boundary, it gave me a purpose. When I think of how I wrote before Therapiece I think I was a dictatorial writer. Now I write because I want to share the result, and that those I share the result with, be pleased. 4-Mar-20

I've sent you some of the writings in separate emails. I've no idea how you'll use them, but you're welcome to use them.

Therapiece. When I read what I'd written I loved the writer, her honesty, and goodness. So I guess Therapiece helps me lové myself, to love a new facet of myself. I so much love its safety. I appreciate the holding you offer. I'd have never written any of what I've done without Therapiece. I need support to access my creativity. Therapiece gives that generously. It is generous in all its ways, even its careful app, and now non app.

Therapiece is, for me, as much about the process as it is about my writing. The combination of giving time to myself, being heard by others, exploring my feelings, being both encouraged and challenged by other participants, being held by the unconditional energy of the group, through the medium of writing, all help contribute to increased creativity and a greater sense of well-being. I always feel different at the end of a session, more relaxed yet energised, less insular, and better for having expressed myself.

Sometimes, given a prompt or an exercise, no clear ideas come to mind immediately. At times I might sit quietly for a few minutes, or doodle, until an idea emerges. Or I might play with a question, leaving an answer to come through the writing. Stream of consciousness writing features quite highly, making no apparent sense to anyone listening or indeed myself, but leaving me with a sense of release, of letting go, of having touched something that I didn't even know existed.

Looking over my notes from the last year I am surprised at how many different forms of writing I have attempted – story telling, poems, magical realism, non-fiction, haikus. Not as an intention but from being inspired by the writing of other members of Therapiece. And with the different approaches came new insights and discoveries about myself and my writing. I allowed myself to gently experiment with entirely new genres that resulted in a playfulness and joy that I would never have expected!

After one meeting, where a participant admitted to something he found embarrassing, I found myself writing my own poem (Secret Shame) in which sharing my vulnerability unleashed something very profound in me, and inspired me to read it out to the group the following session. Hearing words read out loud in front of others can have a very powerful impact, both for the reader and the listeners.

Over the last year I have become more assertive and discerning in establishing what sort of 'contract' I want in my author's time, sometimes asking for periods of silence to fully take in what was being asked and my response to that, and at others asking others to jump in with comments and questions. It was a sort of freedom but within boundaries. And I feel that this increase in self-confidence has spilled out into other areas of my life, enabling me to speak out more without fear of other's opinions. I have become more aware of how important it is to share and to verbalise what is going on for me, rather than withdraw and invalidate my unique experience and expression.

For anyone wondering whether Therapiece is for them I would suggest giving it a try. You don't have to be good at writing, you don't have to share if you don't want to, and you decide how to spend the time you have with the group. And hearing other's words and experiences can be invaluable in itself. CF

Review of Therapiece Art in the Moment.
By Wakako 5-Apr-22

The first time, I joined the Therapiece Art "Pilot", I was totally relaxed and enjoyed it from deep down in my mind because it is never asking for skills.
I've joined twice so far, one time was doing drawing in 2D, another time we did 3D sculpture with nice soft texture clay.
I haven't done art for ages, so I felt so satisfactory when I was absolutely into being creative for something which really connected at the moment of my emotion.

By visualising into a creation, can share my feelings more clearly with others during the session and discover unique perspectives which I would never realise on my own. But also I can resonate with friends' arts and aspects which often widen my imagination and gives me new sights in some way.

At the end of each meeting, it brings me light hearted as well as enables building my confidence to interact in the group.

Therapiece: Terms & Conditions and Safeguarding Policy

These terms and conditions outline the rules for the use of Therapiece located at www.therapiece.org. This website operates to facilitate the Aims and Objectives of Therapiece and ensure the Ethos of Therapiece is followed by all its members. The idea is to use an App developed by a charity to support all those who join. By using the TherapieceApp you are agreeing to these principles.

Therapiece is a project aimed at encouraging creativity within a therapeutic framework. Based on peer-to-peer principles, equal time and author in charge, it is geared to helping people meet their emotional needs and strengthen their human resources. One of the principle concepts is trust through the maintenance of small groups.

When you join Therapiece you join a Small Society. If you are a resident of the UK then you join the UK Small Society. Please see our privacy policy on how your information is kept and used. The Therapiece.org website is run by the Small Society who are governed by the Small Society's constitution. As a Small Society we request your home address but this is optional.

All payments to the Small Society are donations. As of December 2020 the suggested donation is £40 per year but this will be revised from time to time and published here. If you are not able to donate at this level then we will try to find alternative funding. The objective is to cover all internet meetings and website running costs from the member donations. Donations made to the Small Society are non-refundable. Members are also encouraged to contribute through volunteering or working for the Small Society.

The Therapiece website does not provide any other service than to facilitate these meetings and provide the internet meeting method (currently through Zoom). Those that meet in a physical location will pay for the room hire in addition year donation.

Safeguarding

Therapiece has developed the following safeguarding policy and if you join Therapiece you must ensure it is followed:-

> 1) A self-based assessment of wellness in particular based on the level of your attention.
> 2) Support from assessment by peers in the member's group through the meeting feedback - in particular asking if the Ethos was followed - this opportunity should be in every closing circle.
> 3) Action through leaving a meeting and/or taking a break from Therapiece if you feel our safeguarding policy has not been followed.
> 4) For every meeting there will be optional feedback on the TherapieceApp - this should include a specific question about the ethos and safeguarding - "Was the Therapiece Safeguarding Policy followed?" §

Any Safeguarding issue should be reported as soon as possible via the website page
https://therabooking.therapiece.org/index.php/safeguarding/

The Trustees of the Friends of Therapiece will review all optional feedback and consult with the membership if any additional action is required. In this process the member will be informed. If a member requests to move to a new group the Co-ordinators of the groups will facilitate this.

Version 3 updated Dec2022

Therapiece.org Constitution

Version 1.1 Dec-2021

0. Introduction – purpose

This document was taken from a template for a small society. In the Ethos of Therapiece it is a stated aim to form a network of people who have a common interest in Creativity. The idea is to make this community a small Social Enterprise with people who contribute in different ways and also can be employed on a freelance basis. This section is work in progress and has not been reviewed at an AGM to date 2022.

1. Name

The name of the small society is Therapiece.org with abbreviation Therapiece

2. Aims

The aims of Therapiece are:

- Use Creative writing and other forms of artistic creativity as the basis of therapeutic exercise.
- To preserve the Therapiece Ethos of Equal time, Author/creator in charge, non-judgmental.

3. Membership

Membership is open to anyone who:-
- is aged over 16 years old, writes and speaks in English; and
- contributes to Therapiece activities and/or donates to Therapiece; and
- follows the Therapiece Ethos in meetings

Membership will begin as soon as the member has attended their first contributory meeting – usually the first in the month after induction and their free meeting. There will be a suggested annual donation which will be agreed at the Annual General Meeting (AGM).

A list of all members will be kept by the membership secretary.

All members must be aware of the Therapiece Safeguarding process.

Ceasing to be a member

Members may resign at any time in writing to the secretary or chair.

Any member who has not participated in Therapiece for a year will be contacted by the secretary, who will then decide whether that member is deemed to have resigned.

Any offensive behaviour, including racist, judgemental, sexist or inflammatory remarks, will not be permitted. Anyone not following the Therapiece Ethos or breaking the equal opportunities policy may be asked not to attend further meetings. The Therapiece Safeguarding process will be followed in all cases of inappropriate behaviour.

4. Equal Opportunities

Therapiece will not discriminate on the grounds of sex, race (including colour, ethnic or national origin), sexual orientation, disability, gender reassignment, religious or political belief, pregnancy or maternity, marital status or age.

5. Officers and committee

The business of the group will be carried out by a Committee elected at the Annual General Meeting. The Committee will meet as necessary.

The Committee will consist between 3 or 8 officers. Any members of Therapiece may attend these meetings. No votes will be taken at these meetings.

The officers' roles include the following plus any other:

- Chair, who shall chair both general and committee meetings
- Secretary, who shall be responsible for the taking of minutes
- Treasurer who shall be responsible for maintaining accounts
- Officer without portfolio

In the event of an officer standing down during the year a replacement will be found and elected at the next General Meeting of members.

Any committee member not attending a meeting without apology for three months will be contacted by the committee and asked if they wish to resign.

The Committee meetings will be open to any member of Wild about Brighton Youth Group wishing to attend, who may speak but not vote.

6. Meetings

6.1. Annual General Meetings

An Annual General Meeting (AGM) will be held within eighteen months of the previous AGM.

All members will be notified email at least 3 weeks before the date of the meeting, and give agenda, date and time. These meeting will be held online (Zoom or similar).

Nominations for the committee may be made to the Secretary before the meeting, or at the meeting.

The quorum for the AGM will be 10% of the membership or 3 members, whichever is the greater number, plus the officers. Votes will be taken as required, for electing officers etc.

At the AGM:-

- The Committee will present a report on Therapiece since the last report.
- The Committee will present the Therapiece accounts for the previous year.
- The officers and Committee for the next year will be elected.
- Any proposals given to the Committee at least 7 days in advance of the meeting will be discussed.

6.2 Special General Meetings

The Secretary will call a Special General Meeting at the request of the majority of the committee or at least eight other members giving a written request to the Chair or Secretary stating the reason for their request.

The meeting will take place within twenty-one days of the request.

All members will be given two weeks notice of such a meeting, giving the venue, date, time and agenda, and notice may be by telephone, email or post.

The quorum for the Special General Meeting will be the same as the AGM. Votes will be taken as required relating to the topic of the meeting.

6.3 Committee Meetings

Committee meetings may be called by any of the Officers. Committee members must receive notice of meetings at least 7 days before the meeting.

Votes will be taken but if necessary can be Tabled for AGM or SGM

7. Rules of Procedure for meetings

All questions that arise at any meeting will be discussed openly and the meeting will seek to find general agreement that everyone present can agree to.

If a consensus cannot be reached a vote will be taken and a decision will be made by a simple majority of members present. If the number of votes cast on each side is equal, the chair of the meeting shall have an additional casting vote.

8. Finances

An account will be maintained on behalf of the Society at a bank agreed by the committee. Three cheque signatories will be nominated by the Committee (one to be the Treasurer). The signatories must not be related nor members of the same household.

Records of income and expenditure will be maintained by the Treasurer and a financial statement given at each AGM.

All money raised by or on behalf of Therapiece is only to be used to further the aims of the group, as specified in item 2 of this constitution.

Where services are provided by a member then the following should be followed

1) Members of Therapiece can be paid for helping Therapiece
2) Two of the three officers must approve the payment
3) Officers of Therapiece cannot be paid
4) A record of all payments to members must be kept

9. Amendments to the Constitution

Amendments to the constitution may only be made at the Annual General Meeting or a Special General Meeting.

Any proposal to amend the constitution must be given to the Secretary in writing. The proposal must then be circulated with the notice of meeting.

Any proposal to amend the constitution will require a two thirds majority of those present and entitled to vote.

10. Dissolution

If a meeting (AGM or SGM), by simple majority, decides that it is necessary to close down the group it may call a Special General Meeting to do so. The sole business of this meeting will be to dissolve the group.

If it is agreed to dissolve the group, all remaining money and other assets, once outstanding debts have been paid, will be donated to a local charitable organisation. The organisation will be agreed at the meeting which agrees the dissolution.

This constitution was agreed on:-

Date ..../............./................

Name and position in group ....

Signed ....

Name and position in group ....

Signed ....

End of constitution this was developed from a **Resource Centre template**

Updated November 2016

https://www.resourcecentre.org.uk/information/constitutions/#sample

DATA PRIVACY NOTICE

Therapiece takes data privacy seriously. This privacy policy explains who we are, how we collect and use Personal Information, and how you can exercise your privacy rights. We do not share data with anyone.

If you have any questions or concerns about our use of your Personal Information, then please contact us the.team@therapiece.org.

We will let you know by email if we change any of our policies.

1. Our GDPR policy statement

a. Your personal data – what is it?

Personal data relates to a living individual who can be identified from that data. Identification can be by the information alone. In the UK the processing of personal data is governed by the General Data Protection Regulation (the "GDPR").

b. Who are we?

We are the Trustees of the charity, Friends of Therapiece, (the Charity) and control all the personal data in 1. above.

c. How do we process your personal data?

We comply with its obligation under GDPR by keeping personal data up to date; by storing and destroying it securely; by not collecting or retaining excessive amounts of data; by protecting personal data from loss, misuse, unauthorised access and disclosure and by ensuring that appropriate technical measures are in place to protect personal data.

d. What do we use your personal data for?

To administer membership records. To help run the peer-to-peer nature of Therapiece. To inform you of news, events and volunteering activities relating to Therapiece.org including events and activities that raise funds for the Friends of Therapiece. All these communications are via email.

e. What is the legal basis for processing your personal data?

We need your explicit consent of the data subject so that we can keep you informed about news, events and activities. We adhere to the May-2018 GDPR legislation.

f. Will your personal data be shared?

No.

g. How long do we keep your personal data?

We only keep current data. All Members and Visitors who leave will have their data removed within 28 days. You must inform us of when you leave using unsubscribe.

h. Your rights and your personal data.

Unless subject to an exemption under the GDPR, you have the following rights with respect to your personal data:- i) to have copy of your personal data which we hold on you, ii) to correct your personal data which we hold on you, iii) request your personal data is erased at any time.

i. What information do we hold?

For each Member we keep an email address, address and phone number and details of meetings attended. For each Visitor we keep only an email address.

j. How do you communicate with us?

Communication will be via email. Please email the.team@therapiece.org with all requests relating to personal data.

2. The Basics

2.A. About Us

Therapiece is a peer-to-peer network of people operated by a UK charity called Friends of Therapiece. The Charity is run by the Trustees as defined in the constitution ("we," "us," "our," and " Therapiece").

The Charity enables our Members to take part in meetings over the internet or in person for the purpose of exploring their wellbeing through creative activities.

2.B. Key Terms

In this privacy policy, these terms have the following meanings:

 "Web App(s)" means any one or all of the Therapiece applications available for Members to use on their computing devices.

"Member" is a person who has joined Therapiece and is registered with us to use the Therapiece App(s) and join meetings. If they are a resident of the UK they are a member of the Charity.

"Personal Information" means any information that identifies or can be used to identify an individual directly or indirectly. Examples of Personal Information include, but are not limited to, first and last name, email address, or location address.

"Service" has the meaning given to it in our Terms and Conditions.

"Visitor" means, any person who visits any of our Therapiece websites, addresses, or otherwise engages with us and leaves contact details (email) with us.

"you" and "your" means, depending on the context, either a Member or a Visitor.

3. Privacy for Visitors

This section applies to Personal Information that we collect and process when you visit the Therapiece Site and leave your details. In this section, "you" and "your" refer to Visitors.

3.A. Information We Collect

(i) Information you provide to us

- Personal contact information (such as your name, email address);
- Any information you choose to provide to us when completing any 'free text' boxes in our forms.

(ii) Information we collect automatically through the Mailchimp facility:

- Device information: such as your IP address, your browser,
- Usage data: such as information about how you interact with our emails,

3.B Use of Personal Information

- We will only send you information about Therapiece

3.C. Cookies and Tracking Technologies

- We do not use cookies if you are a visitor to the Therapiece website.

3.D Third-Party use

- We will not use your Personal Information for any other purpose than for running Therapiece and we will not let any Third party have access to it.

3.E To unsubscribe and remove all your personal information

- Use the unsubscribe link in any Mailchimp email to you to remove your personal information

4. Privacy for Members

This section applies to the Personal Information we collect and process from a Member through using the TherapieceApp. If you are not a Member, the Visitors section of this policy may be more applicable to you and your data. In this section, "you" and "your" refer to Members and potential Members.

4.A. Information We Collect

The Personal Information that we collect is only your personal information and not to do with any other organisation you might be involved with.

(i) Information you provide to us: You will need to provide certain Personal Information to us when you sign up for a Therapiece account and use the Service.

- Personal contact information (your name, address, phone number, email address)
- Account log-in credentials (such as your email address or username and password when you sign up for an account with us);
- Troubleshooting and support data (which is data you provide or we otherwise collect in connection with support queries we receive from you. This may include contact or authentication data, the content of your chats and other communications with us, and the product or service you are using related to your help inquiry); and
- Donation information (including your bank card numbers and associated identifiers and billing address).

(ii) Information we collect automatically: When you use the TherapieceApp, we will automatically collect Service Usage Data which may include:

- Device information: We collect information about the device and applications you use to access the Service, such as your IP address, your operating system, your browser ID, and other information about your system and connection.
- Log data: Our servers keep log files that record data each time a device accesses those servers and the nature of each access, including originating IP addresses and your activity in the Service (such as the date/time stamps associated with your usage, pages and files viewed, searches and other actions you take (for example, which features you used)),
- Usage data: We collect usage data about you whenever you interact with our Service, which may include the dates and times you access the Service and when you attend a Therapiece Meeting.

4.B. Use of Personal Information

We may use the Personal Information we collect or receive through the Service Usage for the purposes and on the legal bases identified below:

- To send you system alert messages in relation to your Therapiece membership and meetings.
- To communicate with you about your account and provide support.
- To ensure compliance with our Terms & Conditions and Safeguarding to protect the rights and safety of our Members in reliance on our legitimate interest to protect against misuse or abuse of our Service and to pursue remedies available.
- To meet legal requirements.
- To provide, support and improve the Service to the Members
- To request donation and collect money for Therapiece funds.

4.C. Cookies and Tracking Technologies

- We do not use cookies

3.D Third-Party use

- We will not use your Personal Information for any other purpose than for running Therapiece and we will not let any Third party have access to it.

3.E To unsubscribe, leave Therapiece and remove all your personal information

- Use the unsubscribe link in a Therapiece email to you to leave Therapiece and delete your personal information. There are a number of options to take a break and receive less information.

3.F. Your Data Protection Rights

You have the following data protection rights:

- To access; correct; update; remove your Personal Information.
- You can manage your individual account and profile settings within the dashboard of the TherapieceApp. You can remove all your personal information as stated in 3.E.
- The right to complain to a data protection authority about the collection and use of Personal Information. For more information, please contact your local data protection authority. Contact details for data protection authorities in the EEA and UK are available here and Switzerland are available here.

We respond to all requests we receive from individuals wishing to exercise their data protection rights in accordance with applicable data protection law. We will ask you to verify your identity in order to help us respond efficiently to your request.

Version 3

Therapiece use of the EN&R (Emotional Needs & Resources) Model

One of the ways Therapiece works can be looked at with this model. There are other models that apply too of course.

This is a Word file that can be downloaded from the Therapiece Website.

Please look at the next two pages of EN&Rs. Please arrange the 9 cards on each page into three columns as follows:-
1) Furthest right column those card that are most important for you to change and you hope Therapiece will help in this area
2) Place in the middle using the same scale as 1) those in a moderate importance to you.
3) Place in the left column using the same scale as 1) those least importance to you.

Please leave the three basics (Food&Drink, Sleep & Movement) where they are. If you need or want to please use green bars to separate the groups.

Thank you!

Example arrangement based on how Therapiece may help fulfil emotional needs

Privacy	Emotional Connection	Community
Control	Achievement	Meaning & Purpose
Security	Respected (Status)	Attention
Food & Drink	Movement	Sleep

Resources >>>--Pls move cards ->>>----Least important –>>>--moderate -->>>-- important
Example arrangement based on how Therapiece may help develop resources

Black & White Thinking	Rapport	Observing self
Rational Thinking	Emotions	Memory
Pattern Matching	Dreaming	Imagination
Food & Drink	Movement	Sleep

Printed in Great Britain
by Amazon